Praise for *Gender Equity in Elementary Schools*

"I was drawn into this book and didn't want to put it down. It focuses on the need for all educators—and really anybody—to reflect critically and deeply on the adverse impact of gender bias on children and its effect on their personal development and achievement in school. The author gives readers a practical roadmap to examine and understand gender-healthy practices in schools and communities that will be meaningful for generations to come. *Gender Equity in Elementary Schools* is an invaluable resource for teachers and school leaders; it can help educators drive positive, actionable change in schools."—Peggy Brookins, president and CEO, National Board for Professional Teaching Standards

"Think you don't have gender bias? Believe that your own gender or teaching experience can overcome any perceived bias? Ready for a challenge, discovery, and growth—just like your students? Then this carefully crafted toolbox is for you! And it's also for those who don't think they need it. Dorothy Venditto's laserlike focus on today and tomorrow's gender equity issue is a new seed of enlightenment for the educator in all of us. Her comprehensive, thought-provoking tips and strategies are valuable teaching tools, created as living documents we all must continually nurture. The call to action for self-reflection that Venditto highlights will lead to impactful development and changes required for gender equity health in our schools."—Dennis Fitzgerald, third grade teacher, Joaquin Miller Elementary, Oakland, CA

"The classroom can still be an unequal space. This book is both an important call to action and a valuable road map for any educator who strives to make sure that his or her classroom is a setting where gender equity is assured and all children can flourish. When the classroom becomes a better and safer place, so too does our country and our world."—Kayce Freed Jennings, director, Girl Rising Educators

"Being the father of two girls, ages 11 and 15, and having the opportunity as an administrator to have seen Dorothy in action with our students, it is wonderful to see her work in a book. *Gender Equity in Elementary Schools* is a perfect blueprint for schools. It assists teachers with activities and resources to create responsive, proactive schools and become transformational in their approach to develop gender equitable schools. The wonderful thing about Dorothy's approach is to focus in class, at school, and the larger community to make change."—Edward Escobar, director, Pupil Personnel Services, Bedford Central School District

Gender Equity in Elementary Schools

Gender Equity in Elementary Schools

A Road Map for Learning and Positive Change

Dorothy Chiffriller Venditto

ROWMAN & LITTLEFIELD
Lanham • Boulder • New York • London

Published by Rowman & Littlefield
An imprint of The Rowman & Littlefield Publishing Group, Inc.
4501 Forbes Boulevard, Suite 200, Lanham, Maryland 20706
www.rowman.com

6 Tinworth Street, London SE11 5AL, United Kingdom

Copyright © 2020 by Dorothy Chiffriller Venditto

All figures courtesy of the author unless otherwise noted.

All rights reserved. No part of this book may be reproduced in any form or by any electronic or mechanical means, including information storage and retrieval systems, without written permission from the publisher, except by a reviewer who may quote passages in a review.

British Library Cataloguing in Publication Information Available

Library of Congress Cataloging-in-Publication Data

Names: Venditto, Dorothy Chiffriller, 1957– author.
Title: Gender equity in elementary schools : a road map for learning and positive change / Dorothy Chiffriller Venditto.
Description: Lanham : Rowman & Littlefield, [2020] | Includes bibliographical references and index. | Summary: "This book supports educators by giving them the language to talk about gender equity, and the tools to assess culture curriculum."—Provided by publisher.
Identifiers: LCCN 2020006313 (print) | LCCN 2020006314 (ebook) | ISBN 9781475854855 (cloth) | ISBN 9781475854862 (paperback) | ISBN 9781475854879 (epub)
Subjects: LCSH: Educational equalization. | Sex discrimination in education. | Education, Elementary—Social aspects. | Educational change.
Classification: LCC LC213 .V46 2020 (print) | LCC LC213 (ebook) | DDC 379.2/6—dc23
LC record available at https://lccn.loc.gov/2020006313
LC ebook record available at https://lccn.loc.gov/2020006314

For Joanna and Kate,
the most excellent women and educators.

Contents

Preface	xi
Acknowledgments	xv
Introduction: A Call to Action	xvii
1 Gender Equity: Essential Understandings	1
2 Assessing Gender Equity in Your School	17
3 Gender Equity in the Classroom	37
4 A Whole School and Community Initiative	51
5 Introduction to Student Learning	67
6 Primary Lessons for Students	71
7 Intermediary Lessons for Students	85
8 Intersectionality	101
9 Looking to Their Future	113
10 Resources	121
Index	133
About the Author	137

Preface

Adults often look to their own world to identify problems to solve. Perhaps the problems feel more urgent in adulthood as people seek to reach professional and personal goals. But what if addressing attitudes and biases starting in the early childhood years could have prevented many of the problems adults tackle in their world? What if children in schools actively learned about what gender means and how to navigate a world that has difficult expectations of them? Imagine if teaching children about gender messages helped them short-circuit negative messages and adopt more positive ones.

Educators might assert that gender is a third-rail kind of topic that is fraught with political and parental pressures. It is a social justice issue that is complex. But what if instead of seeing this as a complex issue to address in the challenging adolescent years, educators saw instead the opportunity to radically reduce some of the complexities of the issue by addressing them in children's early years? Without touching politics, can educators build a pathway to support positive gender attitudes? I believe they can.

This book is born from the spirit of optimism that asserts that elementary educators will embrace the challenge to learn about how gender impacts their students' lives and to make a commitment to learn about the many facets of gender, to evaluate practice in their schools, and to take action to create gender-healthy environments. In doing so, educators will ensure that children who are being taught in schools today and in the future can free themselves of limitations.

As an elementary teacher for many years, I listened to hundreds of statements and participated in just as many conversations that were ripe with unhealthy gender attitudes. Many mothers told their stories about being poor math students as girls, making the assertion that their daughters' academic performance was, therefore, inevitable.

Teachers talked about placing girls at tables with boys to regulate their behavior. Children, who would be angry with each other about any number of topics, would quickly draw the gender line with accusations. Gender stressors were often topics of conversations within parent/teacher conferences. Administrators often saw equity only as a racial and special education issue, unrelated to gender as a unique issue requiring needed study and attention.

During those very same years, I believed myself to be a fairly enlightened teacher. Yet, the everyday behaviors and conversations that were taking place in my school and in my own classroom did not raise red flags for me about being gender-based problems. Like many teachers, my daily reflections focused on interpersonal relations, academic needs, and quality of instruction. Gender was not on my radar when reflecting on my own teaching practice or school culture.

My own personal journey of looking at gender issues had its genesis when I was in the process of obtaining an additional certification for the National Board (NBPTS) that required filming of lessons and reflecting on my teaching. As I reviewed the videos of my lessons, I started to see behaviors and hear conversations among students and between students and staff that I thought were not part of the original mission to certification. But the need to probe deeply into practice resulted in seeing what was not at all visible to me before.

I started to see the inequity in calling on students to speak, about the placement of students' seats and how they provided clues about my own unconscious thoughts about gender. I also took note of how much more confident the boys seemed than the girls when answering questions. I became more tuned in to the now very obvious fact that girls felt so free to shed their tears while boys seemed bound to swallow them. I began to see how many student interactions had undertones of implicit biases, often subtle but real. I researched topics on feminist ideology and about the emotional lives of boys. I worked hard to recalibrate my practice.

Throughout these years, I would still find myself making assumptions about girls and boys that were not born of my conscious beliefs. I wondered how, as someone so devoted to learning about gender, I could also have these implicit biases and stereotypes that were so automatic. I wondered how my devoted colleagues could still use terms like, "boys will be boys" and differentiate girls from boys in a classroom chart, immediately making a distinction that separated rather than united students.

New learning about how the human brain processes information provided me with some much-needed insight. Each of us can decide that we have a core set of beliefs. But implicit biases are formed with information that is hidden from view and stored in our unconscious minds. That information is derived from family, community, and from an abundance of messages received from media, often about gender. We can hold a statement of beliefs that belie our very own automatic actions.

I found independent corroboration about my own biases thanks to a test provided by Project Implicit, a nonprofit organization that is fostering collaboration among researchers who are studying thoughts and feelings outside of conscious awareness and control. They have developed the Implicit Association Test to measure attitudes and beliefs that people may be unwilling or unable to report. A link to this test is included in chapter 4. I would like to say that I performed like an enlightened feminist on this survey, but I did not.

The results confirmed to me that although I have a certain core set of beliefs, my automatic reactions to associate some things as female and others as male are well entrenched. Knowing this confirms the power of cultural messages that are so often unconsciously internalized, I asked several women in their twenties to also take the test. Their implicit biases were only slightly less pronounced than mine. Gender messages are ubiquitous, often harmful, and our brains are taking them all in for future recall and reference.

Like much quality learning, some of mine came from rich interactions with colleagues. Several were excited to look at their teaching practice through the lens of gender health and generous in sharing their observations and ideas. Yet it is clear that for an initiative to have real impact, it needs to have vertical progression through all the grade levels, not just a handful of teachers. It also requires a commitment by many courageous educators to embrace a topic not necessarily mandated, but one which will be invaluable to the boys and girls who will benefit from understanding the power of gender messaging.

This book is written for the courageous educators. Educators who see children instead of politics and opportunities instead of problems. This book is for all the boys and girls who will grow stronger without gender limitations and who can instead feel boundless and strong.

Acknowledgments

Thank you to my family, friends, and colleagues who so willingly engaged in conversations about gender and how we can work together to help children grow stronger. Thanks to Vera Berezowsky, Margaret Rose Goodman, and Drew Patrick, all of whom embraced the understanding that children don't learn through curriculum alone. A shout out to everyone at West Patent Elementary School and Bedford Central School District where I found inspiration each day for many years.

Special thanks to the endorsers, Ed Escobar, Peggy Brookins, Kayce Jennings, and Dennis Fitzgerald who gave so generously of their time to read and evaluate this book and to Kira Hall and Tom Koerner, great Rowman & Littlefield editors who guided the process.

There are many formidable feminists who have inspired me over the years including Gloria Steinem and Bella Abzug, both who mesmerized me as a young girl attending my first Central Park rally in NYC. And there are just as many men, including my husband, Gus Venditto, and my five brothers who taught me about the challenges of being a boy and a man in our culture. It is only through honest conversation that we can grow and learn together.

Finally, I send my heartfelt thanks to three special women. My mother who longed for a larger life and her granddaughters, Joanna and Kate, who stand on the shoulders of the brave women who worked so hard to pave a smoother road for them.

Introduction

A Call to Action

A common school of thought is that gender issues don't emerge until adolescence. But just like many long-held beliefs, this one needs a fresh look.

The development of self-concepts and self-efficacy begins early, even before children reach elementary school. In their preschool years, children are exposed to thousands of images and words that tell the story of how girls and boys are supposed to be. Children are watching and listening, and what they see and hear shapes who they become and how they feel about themselves.

Schools can play a powerful role in ensuring that the messages children are receiving about gender are positive, diverse, and healthy. They cannot control the outside world, but they can counter those negative messages with consistently positive ones about gender equity, at least within the hours of the school day.

This book is a call to action and a resource for research, lessons, and professional development on teaching gender-healthy concepts to students and teachers. Gender health and gender healthy are terms used throughout the pages of this book. Gender is a word that represents a social construct, referring to the social and cultural differences rather than the biological ones. If this construct is healthy, it means that children will not be suffering because of how their gender is perceived, by others or themselves.

Students' development of self-concepts and self-esteem is not just limited to being able to express themselves fully, but also to finding academic success. The central part of a school day is in learning new concepts and skills, and showing proficiency through a variety of assessments. Children who feel marginalized, for any number of reasons, will struggle with the needed confidence to learn or to express themselves fully, thereby leading to underachievement. Building a gender-healthy school and classroom environment is one very effective way to replace feeling marginalized with feeling empowered and successful.

A gender-healthy school environment actively assesses the overt and implicit biases of children and adults and develops a plan of action to counteract negative talk, text, and images with positive and healthy ones. A gender-healthy school environment is one in which gender health and attitudes are not add-on topics at staff meetings, but part of full and robust discussions as integral elements of supporting the whole child.

This book is not a treatise on gender fluidity, though information and support can be found in chapter 8 on intersectionality. It is not a book about girls and their oppression, though there is ample information on feminism and female oppression in these pages. It is not just about boys and their dominance, but looks at the ways boys are also limited by a patriarchy culture. This book is a call to being open to learning about gendered language, behaviors, and practices that can be modified to support student growth.

Learning enough about the gendered brain and automaticity of thought can help broaden a reflective teaching practice. Reflecting on not just the quality of instruction, but the quality of gender health in the classroom can support the building of a powerful habit in the support of gender equity. Knowing that our brains sometimes run at cross purposes, not always integrating automatic reaction and thoughtful beliefs is a powerful piece of information. This knowledge has the potential to support change. All people are a bundle of contradictions as they sort through thoughts and beliefs.

It's clear to see that there is good work being done to reduce the insidiousness of sexist ideologies in our culture. Children's books contain more diverse stories and images; there is an increased focus on the mental health of boys growing up in often toxic male environments; there are more women running for office. But there are many statistics that tell us that not only are these things not enough, but that the toxic cultural messages about gender are ongoing and effective.

In the past twenty years, there has been an explosion in the rate of women getting surgical augmentation of their bodies. Pornographic images and videos are readily available to any child with access to the internet. Marketing to young girls frequently contain messages that encourage them to change their appearance, something that rarely happens to boys. All of these things harm not only girls. They also harm boys by giving them an unrealistic idea about what being female is. Everyone is diminished when half the population is marginalized.

With young children ready to absorb new information, they should hear words of inclusiveness across genders and see ubiquitous messages of accomplishment. They can learn about gender messages, why they are being sent those messages, and the harm or help that they do. They can question their already firmly held beliefs about gender expectations. Children can be taught to be real observers of what ideas are being sold to them and why.

The statistics highlighted throughout the book do not paint an optimistic picture about gender equity for adults today and this is explored in chapter 9. The work of both statisticians and theorists in psychology point to adult life for a woman that is often threatening to her physical well-being and to her ability to earn an equitable salary. For men, a large part of who they are is cut off because of the pressure to achieve. With the emotional side shut down in many men, their opportunities for feeling and fulfilling relationships may become far more limited than it should be. Change needs to take place for limitations to be lifted.

Courageous elementary educators have the power to make impactful change today and for generations to come. Recognizing that we all have implicit biases, even about our own gender, is the first step in freeing ourselves from defensiveness about our practice. Then with robust professional development, new learning for children, and living action plans, a gender-healthy school environment can be developed. This book can serve as a road map in developing a gender-healthy initiative in elementary schools.

The new learning and tools for change and growth can serve as both anchors and jumping off points to continued learning about gender health and limitless opportunities for students. The time has come to look squarely at our actions and replace unhealthy ones with ones that help our children feel boundless instead of limited by cultural expectations of their gender.

Chapter One

Gender Equity

Essential Understandings

Elementary classrooms and schools are vibrant places. Mornings are filled with lively conversations as students hang up coats and run to lockers. The walls are adorned with student work and posters filled with positive messages. It is not uncommon for a teacher, administrator, or aide to make sure a student living in poverty has a healthy lunch to eat. Students struggling academically often receive extra tutoring and those struggling with friendship issues are guided toward positive outcomes.

As elementary educators embrace the whole child and social emotional learning, it is vital that gender equity, and how children feel about their own and other genders, be part of that learning experience. When engaged in that morning conversation, are there students who are feeling less than competent to speak up or to share emotions because of their gender? Are students as early as kindergarten age already feeling boxed in by the social norms they've internalized about their own gender behavior? Are schools considering language, behavior, and school culture as vital and integral parts of gender self-efficacy for its students?

Understanding that gender identity is a significant part of children's development can inspire educators to think of new and additional methods in their daily practice and in their role as members of the larger school community. In this first chapter, before diving into what elementary educators can do, some key foundational concepts about gender, human development, and opportunities for learning are explored.

SELF-EFFICACY AND STEREOTYPE THREAT

Self-efficacy is a personal belief in one's own capacity to organize and execute actions to reach specific goals. It is believed that it can affect a person's choice of activities, efforts, and persistence across the many endeavors encountered in daily life. Self-efficacy is different than general confidence. Rather than an overarching feeling, self-efficacy is specific to certain tasks and goals.[1] While on the journey to developing a healthy environment in classrooms and schools, educators who are aware of how gender effects self-efficacy have additional insight that can help students overcome limitations and find success both personally and academically.

More than building a general sense of confidence, thinking about self-efficacy and gender can help connect the pieces between a student and specific learning or completion of tasks. If a student is uncertain about her science abilities, could it be because of a lack of same gender role models? Are my students having difficulty getting along across genders because of learned perceptions? Is there an internalized stereotype that is creating anxiety around a task? Bringing questions about gender into all reflections about students' personal and academic lives will frequently bring fresh insight about their self-efficacy and future academic outcomes and well-being.

There are many assumptions about membership in specific groups such as gender/race/ethnicity as causal factors in skill development and abilities. But the cause and effect assumptions are often quite the opposite. Studies have shown that negative stereotypes raise doubts and high-pressure anxieties in students' minds resulting in the phenomenon of "stereotype threat." Even passing reminders that someone belongs to one group or another can affect outcomes like test performance.[2]

While many of the research conducted on learning and self-efficacy focuses on older students, elementary educators can see the signs in early elementary. Statements like, "Well boys don't like to read" or "Girls are bad at math" or "He's not a real boy" may seem like the statements of young immature students. But they are the building blocks that create beliefs about what children can and cannot do that, left unchecked, may stay with them for a lifetime.

THEORIES ON HUMAN DEVELOPMENT AND LEARNING

Theorists have provided educators with frameworks on behavior and learning. Abraham Maslow's hierarchy of needs asserts that basic physical needs, a sense of safety and belonging, and having self-esteem and respect for others are the building blocks for self-actualization, the reaching of full potential. Maslow, a leader in humanistic psychology, focused on the lifelong journey or potential and human growth.

Benjamin Bloom's theory of learning posits that learning requires knowledge, comprehension, application, analysis, synthesis, and finally evaluation. Lev Vygotsky states that cognitive development stems from social interactions from guided learning. This happens with other children as they co-construct knowledge within the zone of proximal development. Vygotsky believed that the environment in which children grow up will influence how they think and what they think.

Each theory, in its own way, calls for building a foundation, for social interaction, and for the support of continued growth. Each theory calls for knowing the child, respecting individual children and their growth, and helping students realize maximum potential. These theories highlight the fact that teaching children is a monumental task that grows ever-more complex as time moves on. Yet, when reflecting on each of these theories, and those of many other respected psychologists and educators, there is little evidence that the role of gender is considered in the healthy development of children and adults as they grow and learn.

The fact that all these theorists are men is noteworthy when considering the lack of focus on gender in education and child development. Their theories were developed in the first half of the twentieth century, prior to research on gender and the brain and prior to a robust feminist movement. Yet, in the twenty-first century, their ideas are widely accepted in education foundation classes in many universities.

While Bloom's Taxonomy was revised in the 1990s, most theories have not been revisited. Today, educators can update their thinking and application of these theories by evaluating ways that gender adds layers of challenge for children as they absorb information, learn new skills, and develop self-concepts. How does gender messaging influence a child's ability to feel accepted and, therefore, able to learn?

One female theorist whose work is well-known, but not as a major anchor for public education, is Maria Montessori. Her theories most closely align with that of Maslow, as both were part of the humanist movement. "The 'absorbent mind' welcomes everything, puts its hope in everything, accepts poverty equally with wealth, adopts any religion and the prejudices and habits of its countrymen, incarnating all in itself. This is the child!"[3] For educators who are looking to embrace gender-healthy philosophies, keeping Montessori's philosophy within conscious decision making can serve as a reminder of why striving for gender equity matters so much.

Children are absorbing everything around them, including messages about how their gender identifies who they are. Incorporating new understandings about sex, gender, and related behaviors and actions is one of the ways supporting students has become even more challenging. However, addressing sex and gender norms can also be a way to free students up to reach their full human potential—the ultimate goal for all educators.

Maslow's theory asserts that self-actualization is the ultimate human goal. If asked to look at the limitations of self-actualization because of their gender, enlightened individuals could no doubt list a few for each. A woman can see limitations because she's trapped in gender norms of femininity that stifles her creative drive. A man might see limitations because he has learned that his role is to drive toward achievements without regard to many who might get in his way. Imagine if children learned about gender norms as something of an archaeological hunt of past practices rather than restraints on their present and future.

GENDER MESSAGES

Sex refers to biological differences while gender is about the social and cultural roles of each sex within a society. Gender, as a social construct, is in response to culture that includes family dynamics, media exposure, peer interactions, and attitudes in education. Gender expression is the way we communicate gender to others through clothing and hair styles, attitudes, and behavior.

Some people identify as nonbinary, with no strong connection to one gender or another. There are new challenges for educators in addressing the many places where some students land on the spectrum between boy and girl and how, if at all, that should impact their own teaching. There are students who are transitioning and others who are embracing the full spectrum of cultural messages about who they should be.

Children are so aware of the definitions behind gender-driven labels, they can sometimes feel more like a boy in some settings and more like a girl in others. In the video, *Creating Gender Inclusive Schools*, which is detailed in a lesson in chapter 4, a fourth-grade boy talks about how he can't wear purple because his dad thinks purple is a girl color. So when this boy, who really loves purple, thinks about his dad and his color choice, he cannot help but think that it's a girl color and that is unacceptable to like what girls like.

Feeling constricted or gender labeled by something as simple as a color choice is a signal that more work needs to be done to support the building of self-esteem through openness and respect for individual choices. While there are political, cultural, and religious implications for views on gender, perhaps most people would agree that something as simple as a color choice need not be a signal of anything other than personal preference for something of beauty.

It seems reasonable that this boy's dad was looking out for his son's best interest, or what he thought his best interest was. But what if it isn't? What if many of the social decisions parents and educators make are just habit and not in children's best interests? If adults can come to see simple things like preferences on color or clothes as harmless, then there is hope to deconstruct the many other more complex gender messages and to consider their value versus mere assumptions that we have turned into truths through each generation.

Boys and girls are receiving messages from the day they are born about their gender and its related expectations. Society offers up gender-based clothes and toys and families construct expectations of behavior and performance based on gender. In education, awareness of gender identification, gender acceptance, and gender pressures are key in the quest to support each child's academic and personal potential regardless of their biological sex or their social gender.

A plan of self-education, self-reflection, and collaborative action plans can help educators move away from gender-based environments to ones that focus more on individual human differences and supporting each child's individual path and spirit.

BIOLOGICALLY BASED COGNITIVE DIFFERENCES

Educators see the cognitive and behavioral differences in boys and girls throughout the day in the classrooms and hallways and during free time at recess. There is no doubt that those differences exist. To more fully understand how those differences developed, scientists are working to provide definitive research and data that address the many questions about gender and explore the nature/nurture debate.

Just as in the field of educational psychology, neuroscientists are trying to understand human cognitive abilities and human emotions. There have been studies on the size of men and women's brains and their regions, about the differences in the function and operation, and the thinking and behavior as a result of these differences. Brain research is a relatively new science and the results of studies so far do not provide the clearest of pictures.

Professor and neuroscientist Larry Cahill has done extensive research and writing on sex and the brain and his study results show significant evidence for genetically based sex influences on brain function and molecular-level sex differences.[4] A woman's hippocampus, critical to learning and memorization, is larger than a man's and works in different ways.

A man's amygdala, associated with the experiencing of emotions and the recalling of these experiences, is bigger than a woman's. It too works differently, as Cahill's research has demonstrated.[5] Not only is the size of parts of male and female brains different, but so is the function of the parts and structures of the brain.

Some sex differences are evident before a child is born and there have been multiple studies that illustrate the brain-based differences in behavior. A study of one-day-old infants revealed that girls tend to be more interested in looking at faces, while boys' attention go toward moving mechanical objects.

Studies reveal that emotional stories and images activated male and female amygdalas differently and, in fact, activated different parts of the amygdala so that the nuances of memories differed in men and women. Studies clearly show that there are basic anatomical differences in the female and male brains. Many regions of the brain are proportionally larger in females than in males and the way those regions operate differs between the sexes. The regions of a female brain communicate more with each other while male brains are more regionally intensive.[6]

Other research studies look at the differences in male and female cognition from a biopsychosocial perspective. A cross-cultural study of extreme giftedness in math found that the proportion of women in this group depended on the level that girls' participation in math was encouraged. A study of an International Math Olympiad challenge concluded that some countries in Eastern Europe and Asia produce many women with extremely high levels of math ability and achievement with other countries, like the United States, do not.[7]

Some educators might point to this information and see how it confirms their own opinions about the differences in boys and girls. It is difficult to argue with the scientific facts presented. Boys and girls are clearly different, separate, and different in brain structure and related behaviors. But neuroscientist Diane F. Halpern cautions against any rash conclusions on what the biological brain differences mean for learning.

"A completely accurate measure of cognitive ability would separate what each of the sexes in fact do (achievement) from what each sex can do (ability.) This is not possible. Instead, we rely on the only available data we have. But, we also need to be careful about the kinds of extrapolations we make from it."[8] Halpern asserts that findings of brain studies in the 1990s or early twenty-first century are not predictors of outcomes of brain studies in the future.

There are studies that show neuroplasticity can alter the data on the gender specific findings of the male or female brain. For example, research by a team of American and Canadian scientists shows that people can change their brains by playing Tetris, a computer game that requires attention to shapes and visual patterns. In this experiment, twenty-six girls (ages twelve to fifteen years old) were divided into two groups: girls in one group played Tetris for three months (about 1.5 hours each week) while the other group did not play Tetris.

None of the girls had experience playing Tetris before the experiment started. Compared to girls who did not play Tetris, girls who played Tetris for three months had significantly thicker cerebral cortex in the parietal lobe and in areas of the temporal lobe on the left side of their brains. Scientists know that boys have better visuospatial skills and a thicker cerebral cortex. However, this study showed that girls can actually grow this part of the brain through exposure to visuospatial games.[9]

These new studies are exciting and provide initial understanding of the sex-based differences in brains. However, male and female brains are not fixed, but changeable. Neuroplasticity refers to the physiological changes in the brain that happen as the result of interactions with our environment. From the time of development and throughout lifetimes, the connections among the cells in people's brains reorganize in response to changing needs. This dynamic process allows for learning from and adaptation to different experiences.

The fields of neuroscience, sociology, and psychology bring to the forefront the debate between nature and nurture. In fact, with new brain and culture-based research coming out so frequently, it would be a monumental task for any educator to keep up with the latest findings. And when considering how highly charged the topic of gender is, one would need to consider the biased lens with which research is often viewed or even conducted. Confirmation bias on gender and cognition must be considered in light of the influences that culture and politics play in funding specific studies and interpretations of findings.

There are tendencies and skills that are generally confirmed through multiple studies. Boys tend to be somewhat more aggressive and better at math (only in some countries) while more likely to have reading disabilities than girls. Girls tend to be better communicators, more emotionally intelligent, and more avid readers. Girls have better emotional memory. It is no doubt challenging for educators to process this information and construct a day that respects differences while also considering if those differences are really innate or influenced by the very culture they are participants in building.

Some scientists see this evidence in brain differences as an indicator for why more girls and women suffer from anxiety and depression and men from alcohol and drug dependency. Since women have vivid recall of emotional events, then the logic follows that women most certainly experience emotions more deeply. Yet there is another school of thought that asserts that alcohol and drug dependency in males is their coping mechanism for dealing with hidden depression. That is, women's emotional lives are more visible while men's emotional lives are either more secretive or harder to express.

Some theories assert that depressed males are hurt and confused without the language to express their pain and are, therefore, much less frequently diagnosed. Terence Real, a practicing family therapist and author has written extensively on this topic.

"Traditional gender socialization in our culture asks both boys and girls to halve themselves. Girls are allowed to maintain emotional expressiveness and cultivate connection. But they are systematically discouraged from developing and exercising their public, assertive selves—their 'voice' as it is often called. Boys, by contrast, are greatly encouraged to develop their public, assertive selves, but they are systemically pushed away from the full exercise of expressiveness and the skills for making and appreciating deep connections."[10] The results for girls as they grow into womanhood are visible. For men, the results are often manifested in stunted emotions and adult depression.

The biology of boys and girls tells the story of notable differences. For educators, those differences are observable each day. In the journey of understanding how gender influences self-concepts and self-efficacy, it's essential to look at biology, but also the possible biased lens through which it is viewed and the fact that biology is but one part of the human puzzle of gender.

As Maria Montessori knew, the absorbent mind of children is taking everything in their environment. Their brains are constantly processing the images and conversations that they are participating in and are witness to. The messages they are being sent about gender may seem subtle and inconsequential to adults, but for young minds trying to learn about the world, they are all quite significant.

THEORY OF MULTIPLE INTELLIGENCES

Howard Gardner's theory of multiple intelligences has been explored in education since it was first introduced in 1983. Considering the recent findings of neuroscientists, several of Gardner's intelligences would be fitting to be included in the study of gender. Some scientists' theories would closely align with the assertion that women will undoubtedly have stronger level of intelligences in one or more of Gardner's intelligences, and men in others.

Verbal, logical, visual, and kinesthetic intelligences are addressed in the recent studies on sex and the brain and some studies reveal differences in these intelligences among men and women. Yet Gardner sees this as an explosive topic. He believes that interpreting findings would be unclear. For example, women in the West might perform differently than those in the East or those whose environment required greater visual skills might perform with a significant difference than those without that environmental need.[11]

Gardner calls for mobilizing people of many intelligences so that people will feel better about themselves and, therefore, be more competent. By acknowledging the intelligence as individual and varied, humankind can mobilize the full range of talents for the greater good of life on this planet.[12] Rather than see intelligences and human resources as gender specific, tapping into the talents and interests of individuals who possess multiple intelligences will serve people and society in a world that recognizes and nurtures all intelligences, without favoring one expression of intelligence over another.

SEARCHING FOR THE AVERAGE

Even though Gardner believed that humankind is individual and varied, there is often a quest in our society to define the average. Educators may ask, "What does the average girl or boy need?" "What does the data tell us about the average fourth grade girl's performance in math?" Even when discussing differentiated instruction, there is a quest to find the average "high" math student or average "struggling" reader. Gardner asserts that there is no average. As neuroscientists search and discover gender-based brain differences, there is a discovery that there is no average there either.

In his widely viewed TED Talk, Todd Rose of Harvard University talks about the myth of average. He tells the story of a problem faced by the United States Air Force. They had excellent planes and pilots, but poor results. The pilots were not able to achieve the optimal performance possible with each aircraft. After blaming the pilots, flight instructors, and technology, they finally realized with the help of Lt. Gilbert S. Daniels of the air force that the problem was with the design of the cockpits. They were designed based on the average-sized man.

As Daniels proved, there is no average size man when counting for multiple dimensions. A tall man could have a long or short torso; a short man could be broad or narrow. The Air Force realized that a quest for average was a poor design goal and began to insist that companies producing the aircraft build a flexible cockpit that could accommodate all sized pilots. The pilots' performance improved and today, these cockpits accommodate men and women pilots of all sizes. By exposing the myth of average, the Air Force improved cockpit design and overall performance.[13]

Seventy years later, women astronauts faced a similar limitation. In March 2019, the first all-female spacewalk was to take place by astronauts on the International Space Station. Only there weren't enough suits to fit the women. In the 1990s, budget cuts forced NASA to trim its space-suit program. Small and extra small were the first to go, limiting the fit for some women. For the two on the ISS, there were not enough mediums that they could have fit into.[14] For some observers, this underscored the challenges faced by women in fields where equipment has historically been designed for men.

Seven months later, the problem was resolved and NASA celebrated the first all-female spacewalk. Yet the initial response to cut the smallest sizes cannot be ignored in the signals it sent that the average astronaut was considered to be larger and male. The original problem to solve was based on maleness and then only followed by an accommodation for females upon some level of protest.

Both episodes, the 1950s air force cockpits and 2019 astronaut suits, illustrate the problem with looking at humans through the lens of ergodic theory or gender-based ideologies. They also illustrate that creative problem solving can happen when there is a demand for change. How does that tie in to elementary education? It is where this all begins, and what better place to make a course correction than at the beginning.

A school system that promotes human qualities rather than gender-based ones is a school that influences the creation of a world that does not expect people to always conform to a system or a theory and a system that does not limit opportunities because of gender. School systems have the potential to influence a society because from a very young age, people are not defined by what poorly suits them but defined by who they are.

BOYS AND SELF-EFFICACY

When those two words, *gender* and *equity*, come up in conversation, people are likely to think about girls and leveling the playing field for them. Educators see that history books are filled with stories about men, national holidays celebrate men's accomplishments, and boys are born into a patriarchal society that benefits them in some ways. There is no doubt that there is a long tradition of men having power over women. Yet, in attaining that power, boys and men can also lose parts of themselves.

In a school setting, even from the earliest ages, teachers prepare their students for the adult world they will enter someday. In a patriarchal society, males tend to perceive themselves as smarter and stronger. There is an expectation that emotions are carefully controlled. Smart and strong boys and men can show strength, but not weakness. They can express assertiveness or aggression, but not sorrow and maybe not love. Some neuroscientists might say that this is natural biology, while others will point to the interconnection of biology, psychology, and social constructs.

Over the past several years there have been dozens of studies that looked at mental health, with gender being a studied variable. They show that men of all ages and ethnicities are less likely than women to seek help for depression, substance abuse, and stressful life events. All signs indicate that males are more capable of handling stress. However, it's important to consider the difference between seeking help and actual suffering.

If we consider only the neuroscience, we could blame greater numbers of female depression on the performance of women's amygdalas. But with increased attention paid to the mental health of males, cultural expectations of not showing emotion may play just as a big a part of undiagnosed mental illness. A study showed that women constitute 75 percent of those who seek professional help to prevent suicide while men constitute 75 percent of those who commit suicide.[15] Educators may consider these facts when a little boy, clearly suffering, doesn't have the words to express himself or feel the freedom to cry.

IMPLICIT BIAS

Very well-intentioned teachers and administrators who want the best for their students can instill gender biases in their language, seating placements, and relationships with students without being aware that is what they are doing. Behaviors can stem from either overt or implicit biases, and these biases influence everything from classroom instruction to classroom seating and from granting permission to feel some emotions while dissuading the feeling or display of emotions for other students.

Implicit bias, sometimes known as unconscious bias, encompasses the attitudes that affect our understanding, actions, and decisions in an unconscious way. These biases can be favorable or unfavorable and acted upon without one's conscious awareness or control. No one wants to believe that they harbor implicit biases, but everyone has them. Yes, everyone. Implicit biases may not align with our stated beliefs or even represent opinions we would consciously favor. Implicit biases can be for or against one's own group.

The brain processes billions of stimuli per day and must quickly choose what to focus on. It looks for repeating patterns. This information is used for survival, to make inferences or categorize, and feel emotions that attract us to certain people. Over time, a person's socialization and personal memories produces unconscious biases and applies them as the amygdala defines incoming stimuli efficiently and unconsciously.[16]

The amygdala is not looking for fairness, just efficiency in making associations. If the associations the brain is receiving repeatedly send messages about what a girl or a boy is, then the association becomes automatic without conscious thought. If the image is consistently of male senators, male doctors, or male scientists, then there is an automatic association between a profession and a gender. The same associations can be made for behaviors and abilities.

In a 2018 Brookings Institute study on gender bias in elementary school, several beliefs that teachers had about students' abilities were explored in relation to their effects on the gender gap in school performance. With a boy and girl of the same race and socioeconomic status, teachers rated boys as more mathematically able. The study, conducted in 1999 and in 2011, both times yielded the same results. The years offered no evidence of change in gender bias.[17]

Gender norms can play a big role in implicit bias. This compilation of beliefs about gender that are passed from generation to generation often results in reflexive rather than reflective action. Gender norms are different from culture to culture, but in today's developed world, there continues to be consistent differences in power and opportunities based on gender. Men continue to attain more positions of power at significantly higher rates than women, perhaps because both men *and* women have an automatic reaction that it is how it should be.

The "boys will be boys" type of comments are still actively in use by educators. That phrase can hold various meanings. For many, it will create images of boys being loud, demanding attention, and perhaps not taking school very seriously. Behaviors can be encouraged or discouraged by teachers' implicit biases that validate their own ideas of gender norms but that can also support implicit bias. When educators have been immersed in a society that has well-formed definitions of male and female, then even if they have more expansive beliefs about gender, the automatic behaviors may not well agree.

Dr. Warren Farrell has devoted years to assessing the current environment for boys. He describes the "indoctrination into manhood" as often beginning at a very early age. The qualities that boys are encouraged to develop, toughness, aggression, and emotional disconnectedness, are at odds with his human side. Boys are not often taught how to bridge the gap between success and happiness. Many adults, including those in education, are conflicted about how to raise boys.[18] How educators talk to and behave with boys and girls can have lifelong effects.

Consider the only child or the child with same sex siblings whose only early life exposure to the other sex is in a school setting. Picture the girl who watches the teacher frequently call on boys, perhaps berate them for their restlessness but award them for superior math skills. The message being sent and received is that boys are smarter and should get more attention but are intrinsically poorly behaved. Often, the girls take on the role of policing the boys as they witness their female teachers model that for them.

Consider the boy who watches the teacher compliment the girls on their quiet behavior, neat handwriting, and pretty outfits. The message being sent and received is that girls should be quiet, neat, and pretty. These messages don't need to be constant to be internalized so limiting them to zero instances is a worthy goal for any educator. It requires a new understanding of bias, how it factors into teacher practice, and methods for self-reflection to change language and behaviors.

Creating a healthier environment free from biased images and messages in school may give students the opportunity to balance the perceptions of gender that they receive in the media. The average student sees approximately 3,000 advertisements per day on social media, television, and the product placements on the internet.

> Children are paying an enormous price for the sexualization of their childhood. Girls and boys constantly encounter sexual messages and images that they cannot understand and that confuse and even frighten them. Gender roles modeled for children have become increasingly polarized and rigid. A narrow definition of femininity and sexuality encourages girls to focus heavily on appearance and sex appeal. They learn at a very young age that their value is determined by how beautiful, thin and "hot," and sexy they are. And boys, who get a very narrow definition of masculinity that promotes insensitivity and macho behavior, are taught to judge girls based on how close they come to an artificial, impossible, and shallow ideal.[19]

Educators and students benefit from having information that explains this type of manipulation by advertisers and the media. The goal is to sell a product, not participate in the formation of healthy self-concepts and self-esteem.

The Seventh Generation Principle, based on an ancient Iroquois philosophy, asserts that whatever is done today can be fully realized within seven generations. This philosophy prompts us to think not just about today's goals, but to think about the future. When addressing gender equity and taking down walls of experiences and understandings, we can have a direct impact on students today, but on their children. Imagine a staff meeting that not only includes imagining a students' futures, but the futures of their children as well. Educators have the power to influence that generational change.

CONSTRUCTING THE PUZZLE

Each individual child brings their unique brains to school each day, even if they come with male and female tendencies. Tendencies do not represent every individual child, boy or girl. When thinking about the work of the respected theorists, educators can consider the role that concepts around gender play in the building blocks highlighted in these theories. Children need to feel safe as a girl or a boy. They build a healthy life through the support of self-esteem that includes embracing their gender. They realize their full potential when they are not limited in their expression of emotion or in their cognitive development because of their gender or a teacher's perception of what each gender is capable of achieving.

There is a large body of research on gender and gender differences. With the passing of each year, there are new developments and discussions on topics such as sex and cognitive differences, gender fluidity, and gender identification. With so much information to evaluate, sometimes with contradictory conclusions, it can be a daunting task to know where to begin. Along with favorite theorists on childhood development and the ever-growing body of scientific evidence, a good starting point can be at looking at some basic statistics that can tell a story all on their own about how societies influence children's biases on gender.

There are many organizations that have conducted research on young children's attitudes and biases on gender. According to a 2017 survey from Save the Children, which analyzes how grade school children view each other and the dynamics at home, sexism starts early. In the US, 70 percent of girls and boys believed caring for children was women's work and 40 percent of boys responding believed that boys were smarter than girls.[20] While misogyny was more evident in this survey in Sierra Leone than the United States, sexist views were evident everywhere.

In a study by Lin Bian, a University of Chicago professor, gendered beliefs were found to be well-defined between the ages of six and seven. Her study showed that at age five, both boys and girls associated brilliance with their own gender. But among those between the ages of six and seven, only the boys were considered brilliant. Girls had already decided that they were less competent.[21] In most US schools, formal schooling begins between the ages of six and seven. There is no evidence to suggest that schooling is fostering this bias. Yet careful consideration of this fact and reflection on how educators can address this bias may prove to be significant in the healthy development of all their students.

When gender is combined with race, socioeconomic status, ethnicity, religion, sexual orientation, or disability, new layers of implicit bias can arise. Intersectionality, a term coined by black feminist scholar Kimberlé Williams Crenshaw in 1989, refers to the layers of bias that occurs when one or more biases intersect. This is more fully explored in chapter 8.

MAKING THE CHOICE FOR POSITIVE CHANGE

Today's world is filled with contradictions and disparate behaviors. Feminist rallies are attended by the same people who have gender reveal parties complete with bright pinks and blues and celebrations of the upcoming welcome of one gender over the other. Girls watch as women are still "given away" by the fathers to their new husbands at weddings, but also dream about a career.

Boys are born into a patriarchy society in which they are still told in many cultures that they are superior to girls. The emphasis in their lives may well be achievement and winning rather than growth and personal success. It is passed down through the generations, often because of habit and internal understandings.

Elementary teachers and administrators have the unique and special opportunity to create a gender-healthy environment for their students. A single teacher can set a positive course for the year, but an entire school system committed to a healthy gender equity system can influence an entire life's path. Gender bias is evident in early childhood and these negative notions about gender are spread through peer interaction and perpetuated by educators' own biases passed down through their generational understanding of what it means to be male or female.

Elementary educators have the power to make very positive change in educating students about the value of individual worth regardless of gender. This book provides useful tools in assessing the gender health in classrooms and schools, guides for changing school culture, and resources to continue the journey of ongoing learning about gender with colleagues and with students. As educators look to educate the whole child, let it be free from bias and limitations and instead, the embrace of full human potential.

NOTES

1. A. Bandura, "Self-Efficacy: Toward a Unifying Theory of Behavioral Change," *Psychological Review* 84 (1977): 191–215. doi:10.1037/0033-295X.84.2.191.

2. "Stereotype Threat Widens Achievement Gap," American Psychological Association, accessed January 7, 2020, https://www.apa.org/research/action/stereotype.

3. Maria Montessori, *The Absorbent Mind* (New York: Henry Holt, 1995).

4. Elena Jazin and Larry Cahill, "Sex Differences in Molecular Neuroscience: From Fruit Flies to Humans," *Nature Reviews Neuroscience* 11 (2010): 9–17.

5. "Sex and Gender Analysis Improves Science, Stanford Scholars Say," *Stanford News*, November 6, 2019, https://news.stanford.edu/2019/11/06/sex-gender-analysis-improves-science/.

6. Jennifer Connellan, Simon Baron-Cohen, Sally Wheelwright, Anna Batki, and Jag Ahluwalia, "Sex Differences in Human Neonatal Social Perception," *Infant Behavior and Development* 23, no. 1 (2000): 113–18, https://doi.org/10.1016/s0163-6383(00)00032-1.

7. T. Andreescu, J. M. Gillian, and J. E. Mertz, "Cross-Cultural Analysis of Students with Exceptional Talent in Mathematical Problem Solving," *Notices of the American Mathematical Society* 55, no. 10 (2010): 1248–60.

8. Diane F. Halpern, *Sex Differences in Cognitive Abilities* (New York: Psychology Press, 2012), 21–22.

9. R. J. Haier, S. Karama, L. Leyba, and R. E. Jung, "MRI Assessment of Cortical Thickness and Functional Activity Changes in Adolescent Girls Following Three Months of Practice on a Visual-Spatial Task," *BMC Research Notes* 2 (2009): 174, doi:10.1186/1756-0500/2/174.

10. Terrence Real, *I Don't Want to Talk about It: Overcoming the Secret Legacy of Male Depression* (New York: Scribner, 2003).

11. Howard Gardner, *Multiple Intelligences: New Horizons* (New York: Basic Books, 2006), 80.

12. Ibid., 24.

13. "The Myth of Average: Todd Rose at TEDx Sonoma County," TED, accessed November 7, 2019, https://ed.ted.com/on/4s8O5loM.

14. Marina Koren, "The Original Sin of NASA Space Suits," *The Atlantic*, March 27, 2019, https://www.theatlantic.com/science/archive/2019/03/nasa-spacesuit-women-spacewalk/585805/.

15. Jed Diamond, "Women Seek Help, Men Die: New Findings on Depression and Suicide Will Save Millions of Lives," The Good Men Projects, November 11, 2013, https://goodmenproject.com/featured-content/kt-women-seek-help-men-die-new-findings-on-depression-and-suicide-will-save-millions-of-lives/.

16. Andrea Choate, "Neuroleadership Lessons: Recognizing and Mitigating Unconscious Bias in the Workplace," SHRM Blog , December 3, 2016.

17. Joseph Cimpian, "How Our Education System Undermines Gender Equity," Brookings, April 23, 2018, https://www.brookings.edu/blog/brown-center-chalkboard/2018/04/23/how-our-education-system-undermines-gender-equity/.

18. Warren Farrell and John Gray, *The Boy Crisis: Why Our Boys Are Struggling and What We Can Do about It* (Dallas: BenBella Books, 2018), 83.

19. Diane E. Levin and Jean Kilbourne, *So Sexy So Soon: The New Sexualized Childhood and What Parents Can Do to Protect Their Kids* (New York: Ballantine Books, 2009).

20. "Biased Views of Girls Begin as Early as Fourth Grade, New Save the Children Survey Reveals," Save the Children, October 10, 2017, https://www.savethechildren.org/us/about-us/media-and-news/2017-press-releases/biased-views-of-girls-begin-as-early-as-fourth-grade--new-save-t.

21. Lin Bian, Sarah-Jane Leslie, and Andrei Cimpian, "Gender Stereotypes about Intellectual Ability Emerge Early and Influence Children's Interests," *Science*, January 27, 2017, https://science.sciencemag.org/content/355/6323/389/tab-e-letters.

Chapter Two

Assessing Gender Equity in Your School

Assessing the gender health of a school requires reporting that is as objective and as free from bias as possible. Adding gender equity assessments to all evaluative processes can have long lasting effects. They have the potential to identify ways to positively impact self-esteem and self-concepts of children throughout their childhood years and beyond. To make healthy and needed changes to the many gender messages children receive everyday requires an honest evaluation of present-day actions and environmental conditions.

Evaluation tools can measure the presence girls and women have in a kindergarten to twelfth-grade curriculum and available literature, classroom layout and design, visual messages throughout the school, language and conversational tone in adult/child interactions, and adult and child gender biases. Assessing understanding and training on issues of gender equity is a key component in the evaluation process. Within schools, there is a great opportunity to do in-depth research into the many layers of gender equity. Educators would then be able to formulate a plan of action to create a school atmosphere of gender equity and inclusion.

Just as any good unit of study for children begins with an assessment of what is known, so too should professional development for educators. Before setting out on a path of developing a program for a class, team, or school, assessing strengths and areas of improvement will aid in setting the correct path. These assessment tools can be used by a small group of teachers on a team or within an entire school building as part of a series of workshops or professional development. Using assessment tools like the ones provided in this chapter can steer a team away from anecdotal evidence and towards objective information that can serve as a foundational tool.

Each assessment's name begins with "L&L" as a reminder of the mission at hand. The assessment tools are used during Listening and Looking Tours. Assessors should be listening to conversations and looking at the school and classroom environment and behaviors without judgment, just reporting. These assessments can be used as is or modified for individual schools and their specific needs.

The information gleaned from the *L&L Classroom Layout and Design Survey* will guide you to a greater understanding of how even the most subtle arrangements might be sending messages. Perhaps you will see a room with posters with inspirational messages or one with posters of little-known female scientists. The observations made about the cluster of boys and girls may lead to further questions.

Classroom teachers can be asked about their own reasoning and beliefs behind their process and classroom layout. Are they positioning students of specific gender for classroom management to make their day go more smoothly or for diversity of gender and conversation? Or is seating of students arranged to complement strengths, regardless of gender but instead to facilitate deeper learning?

When reviewing the assessments and evaluations, be mindful of all the observations and conversations that take place during a postassessment discussion with teachers. Teachers know their students and can offer a perspective and context for the information gathered during the survey. For example, during the survey, observers might note that three boys are together at a table with no girls. A conversation with the teacher might reveal that the boys are practicing social–emotional skills with specific skills and strategies taught to them. Or that each one brings a unique skill to the group that is enhancing their learning.

Conversations with colleagues may reveal that gender bias was not a consideration in the seating arrangements. Or the conversations may raise concern and prompt a deeper discussion and suggestions about gender inclusivity. Gender diversity is a valuable focus, but when assessing the gender health of a classroom, all the many variables of teacher decisions should be weighed. The assessments should guide understanding rather than tell a full story.

Flexible seating arrangements that some schools have adopted can offer students the opportunity to create self-selected groups for independent study. Observing how and where students gather can elicit valuable information on study and work habits that may be based on gender norms and individual preferences. For example, if a group of girls have gathered to work without a boy present, one might wonder if it's because they are a group of friends or if there is a reason that boys are not a presence in the group.

Several studies have shown that physically, boys tend to be more active than girls and can become more restless if they have to sit for long periods.

Some girls are also very active and need break periods from long periods sitting. The philosophy of pairing less active students in an attempt to more positively influence the more active students doesn't facilitate the self-esteem or the focus of either group. When pairing students to control behavior, the result often is a group of girls who are less active trying to police the boy's more active behaviors. This does not promote gender-healthy relationships and it often isn't effective.

Regardless of gender, classroom design should meet the needs of students across gender and learning styles. Differentiation can be extended beyond curriculum to include the physical layout of classrooms and schools. More effective classroom design can be developed with consideration given to the biological differences in children, without gender assumptions but with individual needs in mind. The use of this assessment is to uncover what was not seen before in classroom design.

Using this classroom layout and design survey can facilitate more careful observations of the movement around the classroom. Seeing various groupings and sharing observations with students can be an opportunity for class discussions on not only gender, but inclusion and self-awareness. In a flexible seating classroom, girls and boys might be seeking each other out because they've learned something new to appreciate about each other. While this assessment is intended to strengthen practice, it need not only be the teacher who modifies behavior. Sharing findings with students can lead to their own self-reflection and growth.

In the *L&L Curriculum/Literature Survey*, educators are guided to evaluate the gender representation within the written word. It is not surprising that many textbooks and content materials are comprised of more stories about males than females. Particularly in social studies and science, men are the noted leaders, with women given honorable mentions for their little-known contributions.

Historically, opportunities for women in leadership roles have been minimal, so their underrepresentation may seem inevitable. An assessment can help educators determine how much of a correction needs to be addressed. Many teachers themselves are unaware of the enormous contributions made by women. Articles, books, and films on women's impact on our society can be found in chapter 10 of this book for teachers to use for their own professional development or within classroom lessons.

Another common way to address inequities is to focus on girls and women during Women's History Month and to celebrate the International Day of the Girl. These movements and events were created to right past wrongs and to focus on the accomplishments and contributions by women. They are valuable stand-alone opportunities. However, knowing the value of interdisciplinary and integrated studies, educators will hopefully also see the impor-

L&L Classroom Layout and Design Survey

Today's Date: _____

Grade Level: _____ Teacher: _____

Observer: _____ Title: _____

Observations

Seating Layout (Check one or more)

Desks: _____ Tables: _____ Flexible Seating: _____

Seats: (Check one) Assigned ___ Student Selected: ____

Seating by gender (Describe in detail. Examples: Mix of girls and boys at each table/Varies throughout room/Girls and boys segregated by gender.

_____
_____
_____
_____

Displays/Posters

Gender Neutral: _____

Gender Specific: _____ Male _____ Female ___

_____
_____

Figure 2.1. L&L Classroom Layout/Design Survey

tance of regular acknowledgment and teaching of the contributions of women beyond just specific months or days.

Assessing the quality of books in the classroom and school library is an ambitious task but one that can reveal the messages sent to boys and girls on gender. Questions to consider while doing an assessment include not only the number of boys and girls as main characters in classroom literature, but also the quality of interactions, traditional versus contemporary roles, and the representation of girls and boys from various races and ethnicities. Conducting this type of assessment can also offer the chance to dive deeper into the overall quality of literature for not only its messages about gender but about real life struggles that are age appropriate.

Reviewing content material and classroom literature is a time-consuming task. To ensure that a thorough evaluation takes place, a schedule of reviewers and material to be reviewed should be developed. The survey is a guide but cannot encompass all that teachers and administrators might need to assess. As the process of evaluation goes on, other areas of concern may arise. Initially, one might consider other questions such as how many times that girls or women are central characters, whether that be in a math word problem, social studies text, or example of scientific inquiry. However, as they move on, educators have the opportunity to dig deeper and go beyond numbers and to consider more than just frequency.

Evaluators have the opportunity to consider how boys and girls and men and women are portrayed. Behaviors, interpersonal relationships, and the emotional and intellectual lives of specific genders all have impactful roles on how children begin to internalize their own assessment of gender and its related value. These types of observations may not fit into a checklist but are important and valuable pieces of information to take note of for a broader discussion during curriculum meetings.

Numbers do tell a story. The fact that a social studies text has more men than women is a good checklist item. Yet there is more to consider about the influence of these stories. If many of the girls in a textbook are relegated to a limited and outdated stereotype, the story takes precedence over the numbers. If boys and men in social studies texts are filled with heroes who accomplish much but feel little, what message do these ubiquitous stories tell about what it means to be a boy and a man? As is often the case with surveys and evaluations, the picture becomes clearer as more work is done and with that, the goal of equity draws closer.

Using the *L&L Language and Behavior Survey*, educators can take note of language and behavior that stands out as being gender centered. Making a determination about the language and behaviors led by teachers in a classroom is best done over a series of several observations and at different times of the day. Instructional, transitional, and free time periods can prompt different discoveries where boys and girls are addressed as students vs. students

L&L Curriculum/Literature Survey
Sheet 1

Today's Date: _____

Subject Area: _____   Grade: _____

Unit of Study: _____

Female Representation in Curriculum Text

Girls/Women as central feature/character: (check one)

Less than 10%   _____

Less than 25%   _____

Less than 50%   _____

More than 50%   _____

Females as Title Character in Classroom Literature

Less than 10%   _____

Less than 25%   _____

Less than 50%   _____

More than 50%   _____

Figure 2.2. L&L Curriculum and Literature Survey

L&L Curriculum/Literature Survey

Sheet 2

Directions: Randomly select twenty books from the classroom library to review. Take note of the following in a notebook or on computer. If you have additional questions related to gender, include them in your response.

Note: Working with a team member will allow for easier facilitation of this survey.

1. Is the lead character(s) a boy or girl?
2. What problem is the lead attempting to solve?
3. What emotions does the character express?
   Please be specific. Answers might include: sorrow, sympathy, anger, happiness, joy.
4. Is role does the character assume?
   Please be specific: Answers might include: Leader, follower, supporter, friend.
5. Are the boys and girls in this book doing activities together or separately?

After completing all book reviews, check one:

_____ This classroom library has books that represent diverse gender groups that display varying roles and emotions.

_____ This classroom library would benefit from more current books that represent girls and boys involved in wider variety of roles and a wider variety of emotions displayed.

Figure 2.3. L&L Curriculum/Literature Survey, Sheet 2

of a specific gender or when their value as a specific gender is noted through additional attention or praise.

One type of behavior that is common in elementary schools is separating boys and girls when lining up to go to lunch or to an art or music class. Teachers may announce that they are pleased with the girls' line or boys' line or ask one group to lead and the other to follow. The message that this sends is that these two groups should be separated, leaving the reason for this unclear. In a school that is striving for a gender-healthy environment, a reconsideration of these types of policies will result in a greater attention to treating children as individuals rather than as gender isolated groups.

Several studies have reported findings that boys are called to answer questions more frequently than girls. Classroom observers can consider this and assess the various causes that should become evident throughout the observation. Are the boys louder or seated in front of the teacher more frequently? Or are there other underlying reasons, such as bias? This language and behavior assessment together with the educator self-reflection survey can lead teachers to a greater understanding of this type of imbalance.

In addition to this survey, a practice of regular filming of lessons is an effective way to evaluate words used in teaching and both overt and subtle behaviors. While this process has the potential to provide a great deal of insight into teaching practice, it can also highlight student interactions that are fueled by the classroom environment. Filming across subject areas and from year to year can be an inspirational process for educators and administrators to track growth over time and across disciplines.

The *L&L Educator Self-Reflection Survey* tool can be taken before and after gender equity studies and workshops. While teachers and administrators come to their roles equipped with a thorough understanding of child psychology across developmental stages, their training often does not include a thorough understanding of cultural norms around issues of gender and how to promote gender equity in the classroom. The use of this survey provides entry to a process of self-reflection about educators' basic knowledge and metacognition in this area and as a vehicle to measure growth over time.

The first part of the survey asks educators to rate their interactions with students and the degree to which it is free from gender bias. It should be expected that most teachers taking the survey would select "most of the time" and, if they could, would write in "all of the time." As educators go through the learning process during professional development and learn about unconscious or implicit bias, another go-round of the survey may well yield different answers.

Another area of focus is why a study of gender in an elementary school matters at all. Gauging participants' investment in the work at hand is important information. Grouping uninvested evaluator participants will yield very different results than grouping invested evaluators or a mix of both groups.

L&L Instructional Language/Behaviors Survey

Today's Date: _____

Teacher's Name: _____

Area of Study: _____

Language

Class is addressed by gender: yes _____ no _____

(Example: "Boys and Girls, it's time for math now.")

Tone varies in addressing boys/girls: yes _____ no _____

Notes:

_____

_____

_____

_____

Morning/Afternoon Routine Observation. Take note of nature of conversation between female/male students and teachers and assistants. Take note in notebook or computer.

Behavior

Students are lined up by gender: yes _____ no _____

How many boys were called on to speak? _____

How many girls were called on to speak? _____

Figure 2.4. Instructional Language/Behaviors Survey

Confirmation bias (seeking answers you already believe) needs to be considered in this research process.

The assessment of personal study of gender equity has a twofold purpose. It can elucidate either formal or interest-based learning on the topic. Staff members with a strong background in gender study, either independent or formal, may serve as good resources in professional development. This information can also give a baseline for how much new learning is required and form the basis for the development of a gender education action plan.

DIFFERENTIATING ASSESSMENT SHEETS

The Listening and Looking Assessments are models and examples of what may be used in classrooms and throughout the school. Consider modifying these assessments to more closely align with specific school goals on gender health or add questions to gather more information. When an entire team or school is being evaluated, it is key that everyone use the same materials for consistency in reporting so that subsequent conversations use the same types of baseline data and information.

A very typical after recess event is a gathering of students around the teacher's desk to report that the boys were being rude or the girls were teasing us. If the classroom teacher is not at recess, which he or she very often is not, it requires secondhand eyewitness accounts by another teacher or assistant who was there. Having a form to rely on that prompts factual information rather than casual reporting will serve as a reliable accounting.

If this is a gender-based issue (i.e., boys monopolizing the basketball, girls yelling at the boys) then accurate reporting is vital. The person reporting back the recess events may very well give vague and often biased reporting. "The boys didn't want to stop playing basketball" or "The girls were telling the boys what to do" isn't really that helpful a means of reporting. Gender-based disagreements can be rather nuanced so starting with just the facts lays a reasonable foundation for discussion.

Developing a system that is consistent and disciplined may feel less school friendly at first, but long term it has the potential to save time and to problem solve to the extent that problems are not addressed on a case by case basis. Rather that they will reveal patterns that can prompt changes that will provide growth rather than a repetitive approach to addressing conflict. A modified version of this form may also be useful with other types of evaluations.

Using an assessment that requires recording the number of times something happened, the words that were used, and the feelings reported will provide useful information for staff members. If the report states that the boys had the basketball for fifteen of the twenty minutes of recess, then an

L&L Educator Self-Reflection Survey

Today's Date: _____

Name: _____

Personal Interactions

I believe that my interactions with boys and girls is free from gender bias:

_____ Most of the time _____ Some of the time _____

_____ Never

Personal Study of Gender Equity

_____ I learned about the role gender plays in schools as an undergraduate, graduate or during professional development workshops.

If yes, please provide details:

_____

_____

_____ I did not take formal classes on gender, but read on the topic because of a personal interest.

If yes, list some of the books and articles you've read:

_____

_____

_____ I have no formal/informal study on this topic.

Figure 2.5. Educator Self-Reflection Survey

equitable plan can be put into place. If the report says that the girls were bullying another girl for not being "girly enough" and that this happens every single day, then frequency and time both become very important parts of the overall picture.

In many schools, there are several other times during the day when students are not in the homeroom. Music lessons, art instruction, and physical education classes have their own individual classroom dynamics. In a plan to fully assess the gender health of a school, it is critically important to observe and react to a student's full day. The reporting of when students are not being so closely supervised is just as important as when they are busy at work in the classroom. The reporting of when students are outside of academic instruction aids in having a wider lens of the school day.

ASSESSING GENDER HEALTH THROUGH CHARACTER EDUCATION

In many ways, teachers and administrators address issues of social justice within the classroom and school. And it can often have a significant impact on the long-term success of the school and its student body. Character education programs are prevalent in private and public schools. Many incorporate six program pillars: trustworthiness, respect, responsibility, fairness, caring, and citizenship. Where does gender equity fit into such a program? It could easily fit into every one of those pillars.

In several of the following chapters, there are recommendations for lessons within primary and intermediary classrooms and for initiatives on gender equity. In reviewing these, educators may see that there are opportunities for these gender-based lessons to be woven into a character education program. Or a simple inclusion of probing questions on gender within the pillars can prompt meaningful thought and discussion.

The following questions can be modified to meet grade-level language and readiness. The subsequent discussions can serve as valuable assessments on the students' points of view about how gender drives their relationships and self-concepts in school. Prior to using character education concepts as a means of assessment, teachers should achieve their own understanding of the impact of gender and students' perceptions. Throughout the chapters in this book are examples, case studies, research, and statistics that can provide that deeper understanding.

- Trustworthiness

  - If you trust a boy more than a girl, can you explain why? Could that be changed? If so, how could it be changed? Let's discuss this.

- Are there any ways you see your own gender as impacting how people perceive your trustworthiness?
- In what ways can we change the way we talk to each other to gain trust? Is there something about gender definitions or gender identification that erodes trust?

• Respect

- Can you name anything that you respect specifically about boys or girls that is just about their gender? Explain.
- Have you seen on social media, in the news, or in your daily life actions that you believed showed respect or disrespect for someone based on their gender?

• Responsibility

- In our school, who is responsible for making sure that boys and girls are treated fairly and with equity? Why are those people responsible for this task?
- Do you think it's your responsibility to make sure your classmates feel okay about their gender? If so, what does that look and sound like?

• Fairness

- Can you think of any ways that boys and girls are treated differently in this classroom or school? Is it possible that this is similar or different than in other places?
- What does fairness mean to you?

• Caring

- When thinking about how you care about your friends, are there different ways to care for boys and girls or are they similar? Let's talk about this.
- Should you care more about your own gender?

• Citizenship

- How does your responsibility as a citizen fit into gender equity?
- Are your rights as a citizen being met as a result of your gender?

Researchers and authors often present Maslow's Hierarchy of Needs in a pyramid form for visual presentation and clarity. The pyramid in Figure 2.6

modifies Maslow's Hierarchy to include gender concepts. This pyramid brings to the forefront questions that educators can consider in their plans to support the full potential of their students.

Security/Safety—What steps can I take in my classroom and school to ensure that all students feel safe and stable within their gender identification?

Love/Belonging—In what ways can I make my classroom or school a space that enables all students to feel a sense of belonging and love? This might include a girl building in a STEM class, a boy developing his artistic talent as a painter or poet, or children identifying as neither a girl nor boy as feeling they belong because they are a fully supported member of the community.

Esteem—Are my students being disrespected because of their gender or are they showing disrespect to others because of their gender? What methods will I implement in my classroom to ensure the building of esteem through direct instruction, individual conversations, and classroom environment?

Self-Actualization—Is gender, and the cultural expectations imposed because of that gender, impeding my students' ability to reach their fullest potential?

FAMILIES

The family is the most important agent of socialization because the family is the center of a child's life. How students, particularly young ones feel about their gender, may come largely from family interactions. Educators may see the direct connections between behavior and views expressed in the classroom with those expressed by their parents. By adding a new understanding of the role gender plays in self-efficacy, educators widen their lens on family dynamics and children's ability to reach their full potential. Educators reach out respectfully to parents all the time on matters of health, homework, behavior, and friendship issues.

By incorporating a child's sense of gender and its value into a parent/teacher conversation, an exchange of ideas can widen parents' views as well. One way to approach the conversation is by showing parents the modified Hierarchy of Needs. Through a conversation about how each level of needs builds upon the one before, parents can begin to appreciate how much of a role that gender perceptions play in becoming a whole person, free from negative limitations. How full schools can include parents in the conversation is more fully explored in chapter 4.

Assessing Gender Equity in Your School

ASSESSMENT TO ACTION

With assessments complete, it is time to consider findings and next steps. These may include one group to develop a calendar and a plan to further assess curriculum, another to form book groups to dig deeper into gender equity, and groups to develop a plan to extend the work into the community. As each school and district is different, the plan should be specific to the

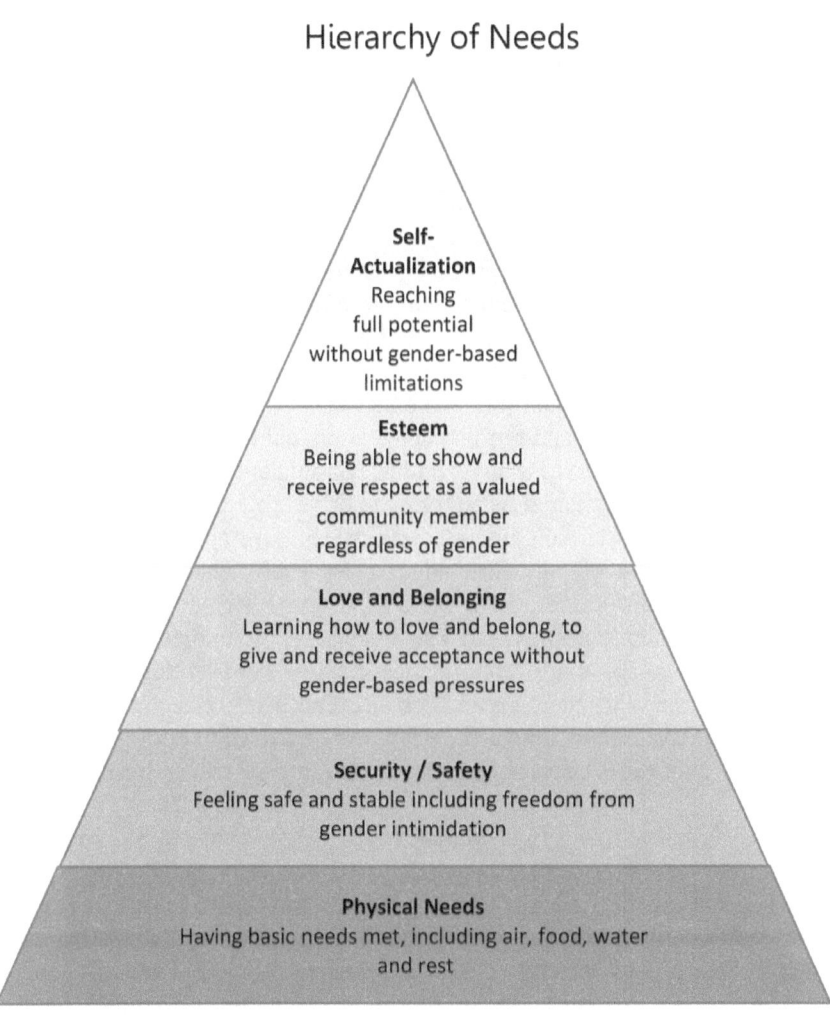

Figure 2.6. Freedom from Gender Limitations Hierarchy of Needs

needs made clear through assessments and doable within available time and resources.

Part of the action plan might call for a new round of assessments to check for consistency, particularly in the areas of language and behaviors. By including student assessments within character education lessons, the program might then be expanded to include not just character, but inclusiveness as part of character building. Actions to look for are ones that are workable and that can be evaluated over time.

In chapter 3 is an overview of actions that can be taken by a single teacher or within a team of teachers. Chapter 4 widens the view to include a full school or district. When considering which approaches to choose, read through both chapters as materials can be used interchangeably by individuals or multiple teams. Differentiate, modify, and add on based on clear goals. As this is done, ensure that everyone on the gender health assessment team is using the same materials.

ONE SCHOOL'S JOURNEY

In one suburban New York elementary school, a newly formed schoolwide enrichment program led to a consideration of how gender factored into class selections and ultimately how the school addressed issues of gender-related equity issues. The enrichment program was the impetus for a new look at the gender health of the school and served as the catalyst for some change in practice. How it began and ran its course is typical of many program initiatives in schools and serves as an example of how deliberate assessments and plans of actions are essential when trying to drive systemic change.

Students in this school's intermediate grades were provided with the opportunity to self-select an enrichment class each semester. The classes spanned across disciplines, from the arts to computer coding. Over a few semesters, a pattern became clear. The arts classes were filled with girls, and the engineering, computer, and science classes were largely attended by boys. While many teachers viewed the attendance in these classes as just a natural difference in boys and girls, a few were troubled or curious enough to attempt to uncover the reasons for this divide in preferences for the arts vs. sciences.

The original goal was to encourage more girls to consider STEM. But as readings and research progressed, what started out as a look at a single focus on STEM turned into a more wide-scale look into their own teaching practices, school environment, and curriculum. It led them to think about how each of those areas affected students' self-concepts around gender.

The first step was to go to the source—the children. Students in grades three, four, and five were asked to take an online survey to determine the attitude about girls in STEM classes. Both boys and girls were surveyed. The survey asked students to agree or disagree with statements such as, "Boys are better at science and computers." They were asked if they were more or less likely on a scale to take a STEM class. They were asked to assess the validity of the statement that "Girls prefer art and music classes."

The results of the survey were surprising. Based on the survey alone, these students could be viewed as open-minded about promoting equal opportunities and interests for boys and girls in both the arts and in the sciences. Girls' responses indicated that a vast majority did not feel limited by their gender and boys' responses showed no sense of superiority in the sciences. But if that were true, then why did STEM teachers have so few girls in their classes?

The teachers in this group decided they must find out more to figure out why there was a disconnect between the survey results and students' actions. They created a teacher study group during which colleagues could read research, conduct their own research, and consider the outcomes.

Members of this group decided to observe student actions from kindergarten through fifth grade, listen to conversations and classroom instruction given by their colleagues, and reflect on their own practice. At the beginning, they weren't completely sure what they were looking for. Rather than devise a prescripted plan, they decided to see where this process would take them. They went on Listening and Looking Tours with the goal to acquire data and stories to bring back to the larger group. They divided their tasks, with some focusing on primary and others in upper elementary grades.

Upon entering the kindergarten wing of the school, colleagues were surprised by what immediately came into view. On the coat hooks outside each classroom hung the backpacks of kindergarten boys and girls. Without a moment's hesitation, they knew which ones belonged to the girls and which ones belonged to the boys. Pastel colors with princesses and fairies and dark colors with superheroes were everywhere. There were very few generic representations. What previously had been seen as quite natural, started to prompt more questions about how young children had already seemed so distinct by gender and personal tastes.

As they entered the classrooms, teachers took note of how all the boys were dressed in pants and usually a cotton shirt. Many girls wore dresses. Those with more casual attire often wore clothes adorned with more princess messages, light-up sneakers, or bedazzled pants. Most students of each gender were already living an outward life in keeping with gender stereotypes. Boys and girls were labeled in the classroom by gender. There was a poster in each classroom that held the names of boys and girls in separate columns so that they could get to know each other's names. The boys' sign was in blue and the girls in pink.

The outward signs seemed limiting for girls and boys. Colleagues wondered how much fun recess could be if the girls' activities were limited by the clothes they wore. The princess backpacks caused concern about their self-perception and the effects of media. Boy's backpacks sent messages of physical prowess and superpowers. While it was expected that these observations would show limitations for girls, conversations with students raised other concerns about boys as well.

Generally, these boys, between the ages of five and six, saw their roles as players of sports and computer and video games. They would play with dolls but only if they were male. Many didn't want to be friends with girls and saw the importance of separating themselves as distinctly different and, in many cases, superior.

The teachers in this workshop group were surprised and concerned after their observations of kindergarten students. Attitudes and perceptions remained consistent as teachers continued their observations in the older grades. Similar trends of boys and girls creating separate peer groups, boys denying any feminine characteristics, and girls' emphasis on physical appearance were evident. Though, in many cases, the princess and fairy obsessions were significantly reduced by grade three and girls' clothing appeared more functional than frilly.

How could all these outdated and stereotype manifestations of gender be alive and well in current day in a fairly progressive school? The teachers believed that the sole answer must be how children are raised and the gender dynamics at home. That is, until they started a Listening and Looking Tour of their own school that included teacher conversations, visual culture, and curriculum. They discovered that they themselves and their enlightened colleagues were a contributing factor to their students' attitudes.

Comments and attitudes that were previously deemed commonplace and innocuous, took on new importance. Conversations with colleagues revealed that many had different expectations of girls and boys. These well-respected and effective teachers were making comments like "Boys will be boys" and "The girls don't give us any trouble." They listened to teachers gain attention of their students, frequently by addressing their gender: "OK, boys and girls" and watched as students were instructed to form their girls' and boys' lines to go to gym or art class. Throughout the school day, they listened to directions and conversations that sent the message to students that they were boys and girls, often separate and most definitely different.

The workshop members considered what messages were being received by students when they differentiated by gender, so they engaged a few of the teachers in a gender conversation. Their colleagues told them that they were harder on boys who cried because they knew that crying in the real world would prove harmful for boys as they got older. They learned that in some classrooms girls were strategically placed throughout the classroom to have a good influence on boys' behavior.

While it might have been easy to judge their colleagues for poor habits, reflections of their own practice revealed that they too shared many of these behaviors. Complimenting girls on their looks and calling more on boys to answer questions were so automatic that it had, until this study, gone unnoticed and unquestioned. Listening to colleagues' classroom talk, prompted them to begin listening to their own.

After regrouping to share some initial findings, the study group members wanted to see if there was a general understanding among the staff of the fundamental biological and cultural differences in boys and girls, how they are raised, and the influences at school. They asked questions about training on gender, the influence of elementary schools on positive gender assessment, and about evaluating conversations and classroom designs as integral elements in students' perceptions of gender and related value.

The conclusion was that no staff member received training during their teacher education about gender and that approaches to differentiating their instruction and conversations were based on their own beliefs and past practices, not on any deep reflection or study.

Continuing in their fact-finding phase, teachers asked for a meeting with administrators to discuss curriculum. They wondered if gender equity was a consideration in selection of curriculum or assigned readings and discovered that the answer was that it was not. The general consensus was that, with so many variables to consider in curriculum, selection with a consideration about gender would be overwhelming.

One meeting attendant pointed out that boys easily lose interest with girls as the main character in stories but that girls were more flexible in what they would read. And, just like Black History Month was intended to compensate for the lack of historical attention to the contribution of African Americans, so too could March do the same for issues around women. Comments were largely restricted to personal experiences, anecdotes, and limited research.

By virtue of the discussion of the study alone, there were some cultural changes in this school. Some teachers began addressing students as friends or students rather than by gender, the visual culture included more examples of accomplished women. The changes made were dependent on a very informal study by committed study group members, with no building-wide commitment to further study gender issues, nor adopt a specific policy.

Despite the initial findings, there were no systemic changes adopted by either building or district staff. There was some satisfaction among members of this group that they took the initiative, but they saw no opportunity to vertically progress this work from grade to grade. A more formalized approach, with clear goals, assessments, and a schedule of meetings and evaluation, would have provided a clearer path and more consistent outcomes for the students.

Assessments throughout the process may have led to a more productive outcome for this group. Completing an action plan like the one in chapter 3 for a small group or in chapter 4 for a larger one may have prompted discussions about logical next steps.

Assessments are invaluable tools that help frame questions, guide discussions, and prompt next steps. Yet, just as gender can serve as something of a box for students, so too can assessments for educators. Just as educators differentiate instruction for students, they can benefit from differentiating assessments for their own evaluations. Considering the school population and particular areas of concern will serve as ways to modify assessments so that staff can focus on areas of need. Frequently zooming in on details and zooming out on the big picture will ensure ongoing momentum on gender equity initiatives.

Chapter Three

Gender Equity in the Classroom

A deliberate practice that is mindful of gender equity in a classroom is well worth developing and incorporating into daily teaching and routines. It is an initiative that has the power to change teaching practices and change the trajectory of children's lives. By focusing on one's own conversations and behaviors and those of all the people with whom students come into contact, teachers can gather necessary information to begin shaping students' days into ones that are filled with gender-healthy interactions.

Ideally, a gender-equity initiative is school-wide. As detailed in one school's journey in chapter 2, a solid plan of action is needed to expand the initiative of a single or small group of teachers. A plan incubated in one's classroom can be disseminated school-wide is a plan worthy of developing. The process begins with the steps a single teacher takes to begin this journey within a single classroom.

Maintaining a focus on gender equity within all the classroom activity can be accomplished with some simple planning and readily available tools. Once the process has started, this gender-mindful practice can become a natural and automatic part of the classroom environment.

INDEPENDENT EVALUATIONS

In chapter 2, Listening and Looking Assessments are provided to support the work of determining the level of gender health in a classroom or school. These are very useful for team members to evaluate each other's classrooms. Yet there are ways for teachers without an available team to use them as well. A most effective way is to videotape and subsequently evaluate one's own lessons.

Digital cameras with full video capabilities should have enough capacity to film at least one full lesson. Obtaining this equipment can be done through many public libraries that will lend out equipment for a few days. For those with a more robust budget, there are now robotic cameras that can follow the action taking place in the classroom. Since behaviors and interactions can vary from content area and across the span of time, taking several videos to view multiple interactions will enable a more accurate picture of conversations and behaviors.

A review of the videos facilitates the evaluation of language, behavior, and classroom layout. Conducting several different viewings is most helpful as each may allow for focusing on one specific area at a time. Using the Listening and Looking Tour Assessment sheets while viewing the video will help produce the most accurate note-taking. As boxes are checked and notes are jotted down on the assessment recording sheets, taking note of any "in the moment thoughts" can be a powerful part of this self-reflection.

To reach a greater understanding of the gender-based dynamics taking place in the classroom, two steps are helpful. The first is to remain an objective reporter during the initial viewing stage. The second is to then use personal understandings of students and their relationships to add further depth to the objective record.

Examples of first viewing/objective questions:

- How many times did I call on boys in math/reading/science class?
- How many times did I compliment a girl on her outfit or hairstyle?
- What is the gender distribution of students across desks or tables?
- How did I react to the boy showing strong emotions?

Examples of second viewing/personal understandings questions:

- Are there gender-based reasons for calling on these specific students so often?
- Through my questioning, what messages am I sending about girls and their value?
- Am I using gender as a classroom management tool?
- In what ways can I support boys in expressing their emotions?

By reflecting on the answers to these questions, one can reveal one's own habits, tendencies, and practices that so often go unnoticed. Taking an actual count of the boys and girls who are called on for an answer can be eye opening. It will often reveal a preference for calling on one gender vs. another. In many cases, the gender that is called on most often is male. For a teacher faced with this type of outcome, automatic answers might include that the boys are restless, so it's important to give them a chance to speak or that there is no need to embarrass girls in math class who are less confident or successful. Further reflection may reveal implicit biases.

Before teachers embark on this journey of self-reflection about the gender health of their classrooms, some foundational reading should be done. Information throughout this book should provide enough of an understanding of beliefs vs. actions to illuminate what is taking place in lessons, actions, and behaviors in classrooms. Without the foundational information, actions taking place can seem innocuous and natural rather than worthy of further development for the creation of healthier classroom interactions.

In some classrooms, the self-evaluations can reveal that girls are frequently complimented on appearance and that boys are counseled on how to control their emotions or other behaviors. For many teachers, the implicit biases may quickly become clear after they reflect on whether their initial reactions hold merit or are just based on internalized ideas about gender and gender roles.

Two of the more obvious areas of gender-based misperceptions are that girls perform poorly in math and boys struggle with emotions. They can be easy to spot and a go-to piece of information to jot down on an assessment sheet. However, when viewing one's own video or that of a close colleague, teachers and administrators would benefit from digging deeper and listening to subtleties of conversations and the signals of body language.

It takes courage to acknowledge one's own explicit and implicit biases. Accepting bias as a natural human tendency can make that acknowledgment easier. A reaction to this new information about one's own biases may include referring to the belief that the classroom is a family and that all the children know that the teacher loves them. That is likely to be true, but it is also true that love is not enough. Students can know they are loved and cared for and still receive messages that result in limitations or expansions.

Evaluating one's own classroom is a very useful process. Self-evaluation and reflection are not only essential for improvements in individual classrooms, but also in providing each teacher with richer context when sharing findings with a team or administrators. Videotapes and detailed reflections serve as invaluable bases for individual change and can also serve as inspiration for others to join in the process.

Even if working with a team, there is value in evaluating one's own practice in addition to colleague's lessons. Rather than being just a recipient of others' observations, the duality of self-assessments and assessments of others can generate more meaningful discussions at a staff, team, or professional development meeting. It can transform a passive and one-sided evaluation into an active and transformative process. Even if the initiative is not school-wide, having multiple perspectives can deepen the understanding and fuel more questioning.

WIDENING THE CIRCLE

Teacher-driven initiatives are commonplace and have the power to transform schools. In a single classroom, a gender-equity initiative may be the professional goal of a single teacher or at the request of an administrator to give it a trial run. New professional learning will take place and students will no doubt benefit from the different types of interactions. There may not be resources like time and commitment to bring gender-equity philosophies to an entire school yet, but there may be opportunities to widen the circle to nearby educators.

The videos taken, along with assessment surveys for self-evaluation, can prove to be valuable tools to encourage some colleagues to engage in their own gender-equity journeys. By seeing that a colleague took the chance to try something new, to take a critical eye at his/her practice and to make a plan for change, the process can feel a bit safer. If one teacher can say, "my videos showed all this implicit gender bias," then it opens the door for others to take that honest look at their own practice as well. This widening of the circle might influence one other teacher, a team, or an entire school which is more fully explored in the next chapter.

Another way to widen the circle is to engage teachers in special areas. Music, art, physical education teachers, and librarians have contact with the entire student population over the course of a week. Sharing one's own self-evaluations and offering to help then with videotaping their classes, if schedules permit, can offer the type of support that is needed and that can build a team of gender-equity teachers. Just as classroom teachers learn from videotaping across content areas, evaluating gender health across a child's day provides a more comprehensive look at the implicit bias they encounter.

For many elementary classroom teachers, observing each other's videos presents scheduling challenges because so many teachers are on the same schedule. Uploading videos onto a platform like Google Drive will enable teachers to view lessons, make comments, and post questions without incurring additional costs. Through virtual visits via free video messaging software like Skype or FaceTime, teachers in schools across town or across the country can share lessons and the progress they've made in the gender-equity initiatives. Creating an online community is an effective method to get thought-provoking feedback for individual practice and to inspire other educators to participate.

ENGAGING STUDENTS AS CHANGE AGENTS

Many successful school initiatives are ones that start at ground level and are often inspired by teachers. However, while students must be provided with opportunity and support, their work can also be considered ground-up initiatives. As educators look to inspire intrinsic motivation in children, areas of social justice and self-understanding can provide a special path to reaching students. It can also open up opportunities to heighten relevance in academic subject areas.

In chapter 4, there are recommendations for a curriculum review to evaluate the gender health of curriculum and literature. But if a gender-equity initiative is powered by one teacher or a small team, the time needed to evaluate a classroom library or textbooks can prove overwhelming and lacking in multiple viewpoints and discussion.

When needed, students can serve as valuable members of teacher's classroom library evaluation team. Students rise to the challenge of a new assignment and enjoy being engaged in improving their classroom and their learning. This is done by simply letting them read books and review them, all with an eye on the characters in the story, their gender, and how they are portrayed. A full lesson to engage students in the process is included in chapter 7.

PARENTS AS GENDER-EQUITY PARTNERS

Whether staying at home or working outside the home, many parents want to be involved in some way in their child's day and education. Many will be enthusiastic about contributing to the success of a gender-equity initiative. Perhaps there are several books a teacher would like to be read with fresh eyes. Parent volunteers can be engaged to read the book with their child at night or on weekends being mindful of the gender-equity reporting the teacher would like them to do. They can answer questions about how many girls or boys were in the book, activities they were doing, and if they seemed like gender-exclusive activities and what the setting is to assess if boys and girls might be depicted differently in different settings.

Through engaging parents in the process of literature review, some very exciting and productive things can happen. Both children and their parents have a mission that is more than just getting the nightly reading done. They have become a team with an important task to complete. The process provides an opportunity for thoughtful discussion in which parents and children get to talk about a topic that many of them would not consider doing before. This exchange of ideas can shape both parents and children's viewpoints.

Literature review has the potential to build a stronger bond between parent and child if the child is encouraged to talk about personal feelings about how the characters in the book are portrayed or treated. It can also become a creative outlet as this family team considers new ways that the book could be developed in more gender-sensitive ways. Trips to the public library can be transformed with character discussions and new missions for finding books.

The student or parent/student team might recognize that not all characters in a book will meet everyone's expectations and respect personal preferences about what to read. Sometimes, children and parents might find it is a good thing to read about all types of authors and all types of people. How much richer the reading will be though with a critical lens into the author's possible gender biases. The goal is not to ban certain books, but to use an understanding of gender bias as another avenue to explore when reading and discussing literature.

CHILDREN AS ROLE MODELS

Teachers make for fine role models. And yet there is much value in letting children themselves serve as role models to inspire new thinking and to form memories of special childhood bonds. Positive peer role models are important because they set examples for others to observe and positive behaviors to emulate. As positive behaviors increase, so too do feelings of self-worth. Engaging older students to work with younger ones can create a community around a common goal that benefits all of them.

Emulating behaviors of positive role models can also help younger children develop an appreciation of values, teach them to set attainable goals, and provide direction in achieving those goals. Most importantly, positive role models provide examples to prove that dreams and goals can be achieved. In the case of gender equity, it illustrates that the constructs of gender equity are not made of hard stone, but of malleable clay that children can feel safe to shape and change as they grow.

Children often rely heavily on social media as a means to connect with other children and to learn about relationships. They get a false sense of what real relationship forming is and too infrequently benefit from experiences of listening to conversations, resolving conflicts, and forming bonds with same and different gender friends. Connecting with older students who have already been introduced to a more gender-healthy instruction and workshops can enhance young children's healthy perceptions of gender and counter other negative influences.

MIXED-AGE OPPORTUNITIES

A common practice in schools is to have primary and intermediary students pair up for academic and social interactions. Book buddies and assembly partners bring very young and more mature students together to engage in academic conversation or to enjoy a presentation in each other's company.

Teachers can expand this reach by encouraging conversations and activities into these meetings between these two age groups.

Instead of matching same-gender students, as so often happens, students can instead be arranged in mixed-gender small groups. In addition to reading just any interest book in small groups, students can choose to read books together that have messages of gender equity at their core or other issues of social justice so that conversations are more substantive and meaningful. The lessons in chapters 6 and 7 lay the foundation for these meaty discussions that will follow among children.

LIVING THE EDUCATORS CODE OF ETHICS

The National Education Association (NEA) provides a framework of ethical understandings for educators. Within this framework are several points that stress the importance of the belief in the worth and dignity of each human being. This includes the nurturance of democratic principles and protection of freedom to have an equal opportunity to learn. The following are a few points that are included under Principle 1: Commitment to the Student. Thinking about these principles through the lens of creating a gender-healthy school environment may raise new areas of reflection that are worthy of consideration.

Shall Not Unreasonably Restrain the Student from Independent Action in the Pursuit of Learning

Unreasonable restraint is a rather subjective term. It might conjure up the image of a student being physically restrained or exiling a student to the hallway when lessons are ongoing. However, within the scope of gender equity, unreasonable restraint could mean common daily events such as the practice of calling on boys to speak more frequently in class. An integral part of learning is interaction with the teacher. If girls are limited in this interaction, their opportunity for learning is being limited. Or, if a boy's emotional reaction to a reading of a troubling historic event is minimized or thwarted, he is prevented from fully experiencing the learning.

Shall Not Unreasonably Deny the Student's Access to Varying Points of View

Varying points of view can frequently be gender based. It is not uncommon for young students to openly express their dislike of the other gender. A common teacher reaction is to correct the students and give a lecture on kindness. Reminders about kindness are necessary and useful. Adding an additional way to address these types of behaviors is to open up a discussion about why students feel what they feel and to educate them on appreciating differences among individuals and groups.

Using some of the lessons in chapters 6 and 7 may help in these discussions. They provide an opportunity to deepen learning rather than subtly telling a student to believe what they want about a particular gender, as long as they don't say what they are thinking. Teachers who display courage in openly talking about gender differences are gifting their students the freedom to express thoughts and feelings that can be mentally and emotionally confusing along with the opportunity to sort through them.

Other means of denying students other points of view may include limited access to a wide variety of people. When inviting visitors, consider nontraditional guests to speak with students. Stay-at-home dads, women scientists, male teachers, people with different cultures and heritages and visiting students can all expand students' understanding of what it is like to be a male or female. Elementary students are getting most of their messages from parents and mostly female teachers and that is wonderful and enriching. Yet, if the goal is to expand rather than limit, bringing a broader world to the classroom can be a most effective way to reach that goal.

Shall Not Deliberately Suppress or Distort Subject Matter Relevant to the Student's Progress

In many schools, teachers are provided with curriculum to teach. However, they often have choice in stocking the shelves of their classroom library and in using online text for reading passages. These libraries can promote the reading about all types of boys and girls, or they can suppress students' ability to read about and appreciate a full spectrum of actions and behaviors of all genders. In many elementary classrooms, teachers write math word problems for students to solve. With an eye toward gender equity, the teacher can utilize nonstereotypical scenarios that can challenge not only students' math brains, but any gender limitations they may internalize.

Shall Not Intentionally Expose the Student to Embarrassment or Disparagement

Separating students by gender, either physically in a line or as a process of classroom management, is rife with potentially embarrassing and disparaging scenes. Consider boys who are called out on the line on the way to lunch. A statement like, "I'm very disappointed in the boys' line" sends the message to all boys that they are a disappointment simply because they are boys. Certainly, not all of them were behaving poorly but the message being sent is that boys are disappointments. Girls may be complimented for behaviors that make them more palatable in the classroom or derided for their tendency toward gossip.

Whatever the actions, addressing students individually rather than by gender is the more productive and less destructive method of action. Calling them out by gender sends the message that it is their gender that is producing the problem, rather than individual behaviors and choices. Shaming is never a productive or kind way to help students grow. Adding the shame by introducing gender into the mix, sends a message that not only was the behavior poor, but it had something to do with a child's gender.

SHAPING SELF-CONCEPT AND SELF-ESTEEM

Two important areas of personal and social development for elementary school children are self-concept and self-esteem. These are strongly influenced by experiences at home, with peers and at school. Self-concept includes the way children perceive strengths, weaknesses, abilities, and values, while self-esteem relates to how one's own skills and abilities are perceived. Gender perception is one area that children use to assess themselves and others.

Educators have successfully adopted the practice of forming social groups to include students who may have been excluded and to teach concepts about friendship and collaboration. By adding concrete lessons on gender into the arena of social-emotional learning, educators and peer mentors can shape self-concept and self-esteem.

An upper elementary male student talking about how he cried at a sad part of a movie or at a disappointment has tremendous power. It says, "I am human, I am successful and I am not afraid to share my emotions." It can make the difference between a young boy feeling deep shame vs. identifying with a more experienced peer. A more mature elementary female student sharing her experiences as an activist, young scientist, or athlete can inspire younger students who, through exposure to bias, may have previously seen more limited paths.

Students' development of self-concepts and self-esteem is not just limited to being able to express themselves fully, but also to find academic success. The central part of a school day is in learning and proving that learning has actually happened through a variety of assessments. Children who feel marginalized, for any number of reasons, will struggle with the needed confidence to learn or to express themselves fully, thereby leading to underachievement. Building a gender-healthy school and classroom environment is one very effective way to replace feeling marginalized with feeling empowered and successful.

ACTION PLANS

An effective means of guiding a change in practice is by writing an action plan. Figure 3.1 is an example of an action plan to create a gender-healthy classroom environment that focuses on teacher practice. Rather than just reminding oneself to be more mindful of what is known, this action plan clearly spells out how often Listening and Looking Assessment sheets will be used, what resources are needed, and other tasks to be completed. The final action is to reflect and prepare notes to share with others.

The last part of the action plan in Figure 3.1 is an important element that should not be ignored. Even if a teacher feels the need to go it alone by starting this initiative, revealing the end results could be just what is needed to inspire other teams or an entire school to engage in this work. And, in the sharing of work with colleagues, new avenues of opportunity and learning can arise.

Action plans may also be used to develop a program to lead students in learning about gender equity. Chapters 6 and 7 have lessons to be facilitated by teachers. However, teachers might also encourage their students to facilitate and to use an action plan when they are working with younger students. In this way, they can see the planning that goes into teaching and work on ensuring intended positive outcomes. The gender-equity champions case study highlights some ways that students were engaged in becoming integral parts of a gender-equity program.

GENDER-EQUITY CHAMPIONS: CASE STUDY

Just as one teacher's initiative can inspire others, so too can the work of students. At one elementary school, fifth grade students participated in an enrichment class about social justice called Gender-Equity Champions, or GEC. The goals of this class were to help students identify how gender affects all people and to learn about gender inequity around the world.

These may seem like complex problems for fifth graders, but as is often the case, students surpassed expectations around what they could process and actions they could take. What started out as a one semester elective or a small group of girls and boys turned into a yearlong club that inspired deepening school-wide conversations. What started out as a desire to learn about gender equity developed into a movement for social change.

GIRL RISING

At their first class, the GEC students watched segments of the *Girl Rising* film. It is produced by the Girl Rising organization whose mission is to

CLASSROOM ACTION PLAN – GENDER EQUITY

PROFESSIONAL PRACTICE GOAL:

I will assess my own teaching practice using self-assessment tools at least two times in each subject area and during transitional times. I will use the results of these assessments to modify my practice. This will result in lessons and interactions that promote a gender healthy environment.

Action:	Supports/ Resources	Frequency/ Timeline
Work with team member(s) to observe my lessons or self-videotape both lessons and transition times. Either team member will use *L&L Assessments* or I will use while viewing video playback.	Team members (if available) video equipment	2x in each subject area during a 3-month period.
Review completed assessments and create a list of behaviors and conversations that may be hindering a gender healthy environment.	Team member, (if available) completed assessment sheets	Review assessment sheets once per week and again after 3 months.
Categorize behaviors and conversations in order of priority. Consider ways to modify behaviors and language.	Behavior List, Notebook to record progress.	Reflect on progress weekly
Summarize behaviors that changed and new learning that resulted. Prepare notes and share with team or school.	Assessment sheets, notes, presentation materials.	1x at staff meeting. Repeat as requested.

Figure 3.1. Classroom Action Plan: Gender Equity

ensure that every girl is educated and empowered. The film focuses on nine girls and their personal stories of striving for an education, trying to work their way out of poverty, and hoping for freedom.

As recommended by Girl Rising, prescreening to determine age-appropriate segments was essential. Two segments about Ruksana from India and Wadley from Haiti were perfect for this class as the girls depicted were of similar ages to the fifth grade students and the content was without displays of explicit abuse. After watching the moving stories of these two girls and learning the bleak statistics on girls' education, students talked with great passion about their need to do something to help. They began their journey of learning, raising awareness, and trying to make a difference.

GENDER-EQUITY EDUCATORS

Through Microsoft Education, this class discovered that they might have the opportunity to skype with Kayce Jennings, director of Girl Rising Educators as an inspirational and informative beginning to the students new learning. Students wanted to invite all fifth graders to share in this experience, even if they weren't taking the full class. To prepare, the GEC students created an overview of the film and statistics on gender equity in education so they could teach their classmates.

These students asked their classroom teachers for about thirty minutes of class time so they could present the PowerPoint presentations they created to help teach their peers. During the Skype conversation with Ms. Jennings, the fifth graders posed relevant questions about the role that geography, religion, and culture might play in the treatment of girls.

SCHOOL-WIDE LEARNING

Excited by their new role as student educators, the GEC students asked to expand the conversation about equity to the younger students in their school. This class talked about the right age for learning new concepts and decided that in grades kindergarten to three, talking about general concepts might be more appropriate than the global issues addressed in *Girl Rising*. The students wrote letters to their former teachers in kindergarten to fourth grades to ask for class time to teach their younger schoolmates. Teachers across the school offered some time during morning meeting or social studies for these new lessons.

While they were continuing to learn about gender equity in the GEC class, they looked to find ways to include everyone in the process. They sought not only to learn something meaningful, but to act as change agents within their own school community.

Students did more research on gender equity and worked with their teacher to develop age appropriate activities for younger children. For grades kindergarten to second, the GEC students led a simple activity about what they believed girls and boys should like to do. As a couple of GEC fifth graders took notes on an easel, others joined table groups to prompt thinking and conversation.

At the beginning of the class, these young students voiced their opinions on specific gender roles such as "only boys like to play football" and "girls like to play with dolls." By the end, through the helpful questioning of the GEC group, they began to consider that maybe there was a new way to think about what it's OK to like and do, regardless of gender.

Based on an activity in the film *Redraw the Balance*, third-grade students were asked to color a generic outline of a firefighter, pilot, and doctor and then name the character. The students tallied the number of male and female names and found that the overwhelming majority of names were male. A discussion followed about why there were so many male names, and about the need to be trained and accepted to get certain jobs. They asked the younger students if there were good reasons that women couldn't do those jobs or if having both men and women doing the jobs might make the job better.

NEXT STEPS

The GEC students committed to raising money for girls' education, so they held two fundraisers. They produced school mascot keychains and necklaces on the school's 3D printer and sold them at school events and answered questions about equity posed by potential buyers. Enough money was raised to contribute to the Girl Rising organization and to the International Rescue Fund to educate three girls for a year.

Over the course of the year, teachers in this school reported about how the GEC students' lessons inspired a shift in class discussions and in school culture. In fifth grade, the class-wide reading of *Breadwinner*, a book about a girl in Afghanistan, took on new meaning, and in a science class, second-grade girls and boys learned as much about astronaut Mae C. Jemison as they did about Neil Armstrong. In one of their final classes, they produced a podcast in which one student said, "We're very proud of the work we've done here. It was important work."

Fifth-grade teachers were particularly engaged in this class with a singular focus of gender equity. But there are many opportunities to integrate gender-equity concepts into the common core strands of math, language arts, and social studies too and to expand it beyond one grade level. A simple conversation with kindergarten students, a women's biography assignment in intermediate grades' social studies, or a statistical analysis of girls' education around the world are just a few ways teachers can help to redraw the balance of educational opportunity and make known the importance of equity for all, right here at home and abroad.

There is often the opportunity to see students expressing their views or creating an action plan to support a significant social cause. Educators have the opportunity, often with materials on hand or a click away on their computers, to support students in their quest for social change. And what better cause could there be than that of gender equity? It is a cause that touches all people and has the power to have lasting positive effects throughout their lives.

Educators can support the development of the skills and knowledge they need to effectively make their case for change. Students can be empowered with the ability to deeply analyze issues like bias, stereotypes, and intersectionality. They can be provided with tools to articulate and transfer that knowledge to others.

LEARNING OUTCOMES

This particular experience of this fifth-grade group shows both the power of an initiative and the limitations of experiences when it is isolated to one group. There is little doubt that the students were changed by the new learning and it was a valuable experience in both what they contributed and what they learned. For issues like gender equity to become a natural part of the culture, however, it requires that it become more globally embraced.

A plan of action that ensures vertical progression from grade to grade and that becomes part of the school curriculum and culture would have ensured that the good works of this group would be expanded upon, grown, and continued. In the action plan in Figure 3.1, the final step is to present to others in the hope that the value of gender-equity study is seen. As courageous teachers or teams of teachers take on the initiative of blending gender equity–healthy language and behaviors into their day, the ultimate goal is for this to become an integrated part of instruction and school life.

Chapter Four

A Whole School and Community Initiative

In many schools, new programs are adopted by a small group of teachers who enthusiastically embrace new initiatives. Gender health is one such initiative. Teachers will do the research and take action when needed. They scan their room for gender-healthy signs and factor gender equity into their decision making. But for a whole building or district initiative, more than a handful of teachers is needed.

Driving positive change and shifting a culture requires that everyone, or mostly everyone, is eventually on board. The key to success in driving this change is having a solid plan of action that is comprised of scheduled professional development lessons and meetings, a commitment to sustaining and improving an initiative over time, and the right people to facilitate its management and direction.

First steps in beginning a building-wide program is through engaging colleagues and staff members in a full and robust conversation about gender. This conversation might include casual observations about interactions in the classroom or personal philosophy on the subject of gender and equity. Below is an example of a chart created during an initial full staff meeting brainstorming session. This bubble chart is a record of the six main areas one school group found to study and to address in their work.

Each school's chart may take different forms and might include starting off with a thinking map, concept map, or a simple list of related topics. The initial emphasis of the meeting should be on sharing thoughts and ideas. By the closing of the meeting, the formation of an idea map will set the foundation for future discussions and professional development.

In the faculty meeting discussion that resulted in this specific bubble chart several staff members mentioned parents first when discussing the biggest

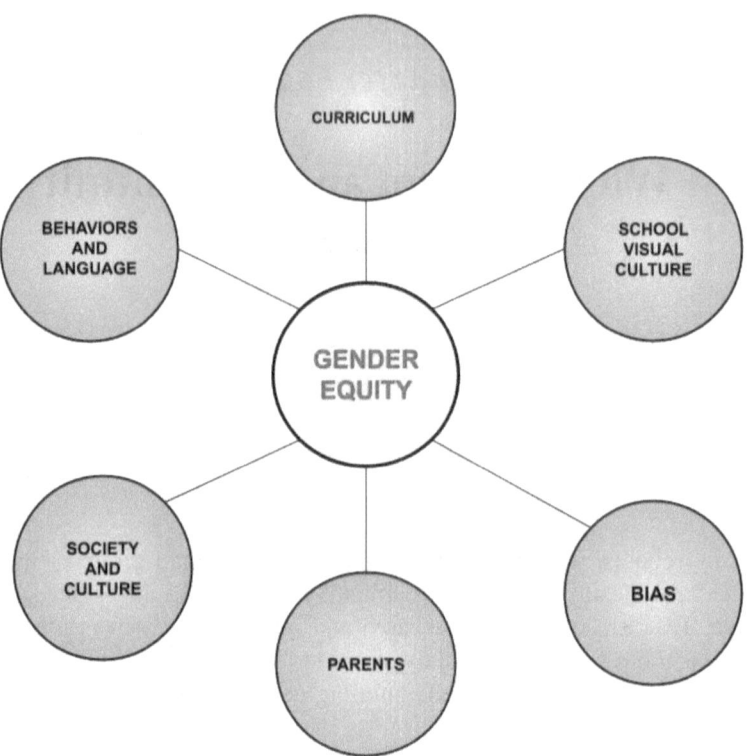

Figure 4.1. Gender-Equity Bubble Chart

influential factors in gender identity and perceptions. They talked about conversation at home and parents as the first teachers. For the behavior and language circle, there was a confluence of thoughts with language and behavior sometimes corresponding and at other times, contradictory. There was emphasis on the need to expand thoughts on this particular topic at the next meeting and the meeting facilitator took note to return to this topic.

The specific form of note-taking is unimportant but it is critical that all participants have access to notes and that each phase of talks, research, and program development is readily available. Creating a shared electronic folder such as on Google Drive will enable all participants to return to original conversations and subcommittee findings, such as this bubble chart, so that as work progresses, a big picture can come into view.

Keeping everyone engaged and participating requires consistency of effort, access to all materials, and an active role for each member of the team. A significant factor in an initiative that loses steam is inertia of membership. Keeping team members engaged and prompting them for opinions and feedback, even when their feedback some may not want to hear, will ensure that team members feel there is valid reason for active participation.

CREATING A CHARTER

A team charter is a written document created to provide the true focus for a team or project. It spells out the team's mission, scope of operation, objectives, consequences, and time frame. The defining feature of a team charter is that it must be created and supported by every member of the team. A team charter dictated by administrators or a few members at the expense of the input from others is not a true representation of the mission. It would then be simply a top-down initiative that will run out of steam the moment administrators move on to the next task.

The charter on a gender-equity initiative might begin with an if/then statement like this: *As an organization, we believe we are responsible for achieving gender equity in our schools and community. If we are open to working with our teams and parents on new learning and to creating a charter that will make clear our vision, then we will be creating an environment for all of our students in which their rights, responsibilities, and opportunities will not depend on whether they were born male or female.*

OBSERVING—LISTENING AND LOOKING TOURS FOR EVERYONE

You may have used Listening and Looking Tours in your classroom or on your team. Now, it's time to look beyond the walls of one classroom. The L&L Survey sheets are the same as in the classroom chapter, but now it's time to bring everyone into the process. Setting aside specific time for a L&L Tour for an entire school has its challenges and may take creative problem solving. Making time and getting support and coverage for teachers is the clearest way to (1) send the signal to all that this matters enough to handle the logistical headaches and (2) ensure that the gender-equity work gets off on a positive and collaborative tone.

The reality for some schools is that hiring substitute teachers to cover classes is not in the budget or that there are other outside pressures that prevent a full-scale observation cycle. For those with these constraints, tours can be done while walking down the hallway, listening to conversations as they welcome students off the bus in the morning, during snack time, or being aware of gender-related conversations from colleagues. And teachers can invite colleagues into their classroom to observe. As outlined in chapter 3, individual teachers can video their lessons and coordinate with a local or grade level team to observe each other's lessons.

Inviting staff members from another school has the potential to bring real fresh perspective. Schools can develop a unique culture and the impressions of an outside educator has the potential to bring new approaches and solutions. L&L Surveys like the ones presented in chapter 2 can provide the consistency of reporting that is needed to evaluate many classrooms. But to fully realize the scope of how gender identity and perceptions influence students, L&L Surveys can be conducted by *all* staff members, including aides, secretaries, teaching assistants, teachers, and administrators.

Note-takers may see that what they previously viewed as basic gender differences is now noteworthy in this fact-finding mission. For example, a consistent theme in clothing or the tone of conversations not before noticed may become valuable observations when evaluating the school culture. The checklist is a start in keeping track of what settings were observed and help focus in on a few topics. In one school that used the checklist, they started taking full notes on observations that included:

- Color and theme of boys' and girls' backpacks in kindergarten
- Ways students arranged themselves at lunch tables
- Conversations among students of the same gender and different gender
- Activities students engaged in at recess
- Words teachers used in addressing children
- Poster messages on classroom and hallway walls
- Conversations among teachers about students

Checklists and notes become part of the shared work and can be placed in either a shared hard copy folder with easy access or through scanning materials into an electronic shared folder. With all this information now available, another meeting to talk about findings will help the initiative move forward. Having the opportunity to share good news, disappointments, and "aha" moments unites staff members and provides information to propel forward to next steps.

Charting those findings can be done by either extending the original bubble chart, creating a thinking map, or a fishbone diagram like the one in Figure 4.2 that includes the main categories of the bubble chart with additional underlying causes of gender inequity.

The L&L Tours unite staff members and give focus to the potential problems at hand. The natural next step is in the reading and research about why what was obesrved really matters.

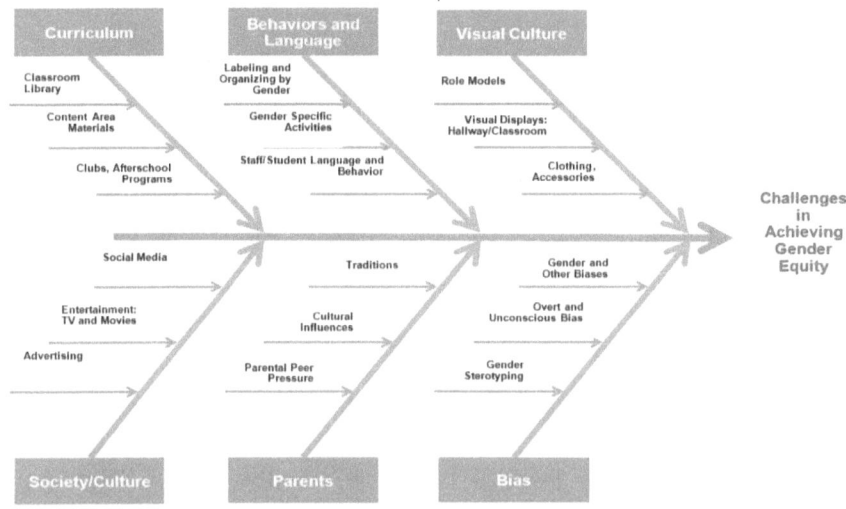

Figure 4.2. Challenges in Achieving Gender Equity

LEARNING—PROFESSIONAL DEVELOPMENT

It is essential that teachers, administrators, and all staff members are keenly aware of the common language and behaviors of adults and students in their own schools. The L&L Tours provide that type of insight. But to understand fully, a grasp of the history, the current research, and the impact of gender equity is also required. This new learning can take place in the form of after-school workshops, during professional development days, or as a focal point at faculty and staff meetings.

Facilitation of meetings can be led by one or several faculty or staff members who are passionate about leading the charge or a combination of staff, faculty, and administrators. Imagine the power of an initiative being led by teachers, teacher aides, and administrators. Teachers with the insight into curriculum and classroom behavior, aides with the unique view at lunch and recess, and administrators who have an overview of building operations. And by including everyone, gender equity isn't a classroom-only goal, but a holistic one that drives real change toward a healthier school culture.

There is a wide array of topics under the umbrella of gender-equity and good research articles to choose from. A general syllabus provided to participants before sessions begin may encourage suggestions about other resources or topics to include. Following is a suggested flow of professional development learning and related activities guide. More information about books, articles, and videos detailed for these professional development lessons can be found in chapter 10. Included is research about the brain and learning theories.

While educators may have been immersed in educational theories during graduate school theory classes, a refresher is valuable when incorporating gender health into the discussion. And for support staff who may have never learned these theories, they can be particularly enlightening and influential in their interactions with students. At the end of each session description is a protocol that can be used to guide new learning. All these protocols are from the School Reform Initiative and full versions can be found online at: https://www.schoolreforminitiative.org/protocols/

Session 1: What Is Gender Equity?

Objective: Identify areas to consider when thinking about gender equity in classrooms and in schools.

In this session, participants consider a definition of gender equity provided by the World Health Organization and read "Sex and Gender: What's the Difference?" by Tim Newman. They will also review the results of the L&L Tours to determine if there is additional learning they would like to include.

Recommended Protocol: "Equity Perspectives: Creating Space for Making Meaning on Equity Issues." Unlike most meeting protocols, this protocol does not call for a set of actions. This list can serve as a reference tool to revisit during subsequent sessions.

Session 2: Creating Gender-Equity Schools

Objective: To identify and understand perceptions of elementary children about gender.

In this session, participants watch the film, *Creating Gender Inclusive Schools* by New Day Film. The film is offered for free through many universities and public libraries. Participants revisit graphic organizers previously developed to determine if additional causes for gender inequity have surfaced or if new questions were raised.

Recommended Protocol: "Making Meaning Protocol." Utilizing this protocol can help guide participants in establishing what they see, what the significance is of what they see and new questions this might raise. The "Making Meaning Protocol with Storytelling" protocol prompts participants to tell their own related story. If time permits, using the first protocol during the film and the second one as a post viewing activity can produce meaningful connections to the personal stories told in the film and then a personal reflection of their own about how their gender impacted options.

Session 3: Why Gender Matters

Objective: To identify behaviors born from stereotypes in young children.

Read "Why Does Gender Matter? Counteracting Stereotypes with Young Children" by Olaiya E. Aina and Petronella A. Cameron. In this text, authors explore gender development theories and the influence of gender identity and stereotypes.

Recommended Protocol: "Save the Last Word for ME." In this protocol, the group is divided into groups of four people to work together. One of the participants cites one idea from the text that is most meaningful without stating why. The other three participants each have one minute to respond to the passage—saying what it makes them think about, what questions it raises for them. The first participant then has three minutes to state why she/he chose that part of the article and to respond to—or build on—what she/he heard from her/his colleagues.

Session 4: So You Think You're Not Biased?

Objective: To identify the role implicit bias plays in school settings.

Read "The Insidiousness of Unconscious Bias in Schools" by Seth Gershenson and Thomas S. Dee. This article focuses on older children, but elementary teachers can easily place themselves and their students in corresponding roles and situations.

Recommended Protocol: "Consultancy Protocol." This protocol helps participants develop the capacity to see and describe dilemmas. In this case, the dilemma is unconscious bias. If it is unconscious, what is one to do about it? The text offers some good solutions and through this protocol, participants can consider assumptions, behaviors, and practices to address unconscious bias in their classrooms and schools.

Required Extension Activity: All participants are assigned to take the Implicit Bias Test on the Harvard University site. There are two gender-related tests. One is about gender and science and the other is about gender and careers. Select one that you wish participants to take. All participants will report their score and write a reflection or prepare to discuss at the next meeting. You can find the test here: https://implicit.harvard.edu/implicit/takeatest.html.

Session 5: In Real Life

Objective: To identify the real-life implications of bias in gender equity.

In this session, both "Inspire the Future—Redraw the Balance" and "The Danger of a Single Story" are viewed in succession. Ask participants to consider the new learning that has taken place over the last several sessions and consider the stories told in the two videos seen in the current session.

Recommended Protocol: "Gap Analysis Protocol." Ask participants to think about one belief on the topic of gender equity that is important to them and to spend a few minutes thinking about how this belief is visible and present in their current practice. Next, reflect on what gaps there are between that belief and current practice. Write a short description of where beliefs and practice are aligned and where there are gaps. Share with small or whole group after writing is complete.

Session 6: Single-Gender Schools and Teachers

Objective: To identify advantageous components of single gender education.

In this session, participations will read "The Extraordinary Relevance of Girl's Schools" by Elizabeth F. Cleary and "The Boys at the Back" by Christina Hoff Sommers.

Recommended Protocol: "Nested Conversations." Participants will be divided into three groups. Each group will be assigned a question to think about and answer. After all groups have had time to take notes, they will discuss implications of findings for individual or collective practice.

Recommended Questions:

1. In what ways, if any, are girl's schools relevant?
2. In what ways, if any, are educational policies and practices harming boys?
3. What initial steps should be taken to mitigate the achievement gaps in mixed-gender schools?

Session 7: When It's Not Just about Gender

Objective: To identify the effects of intersectionality: gender equity and another form of bias.

In this session, participants will watch two short films. The first "Intersectionality 101" and the second "The Urgency of Intersectionality" in which Kimberlé Crenshaw, who created the term *intersectionality*, provides graphic examples of the outcomes when people face both racial and gender bias. The ending minutes are graphic and you might choose to show the beginning of the video only. Prescreening is recommended.

Recommended Protocol: "Peeling the Onion." In this protocol the facilitator describes the problem/dilemma (as outlined in the films) and asks a question to help focus the group's responses. Then clarifying questions from group members to the presenter are asked. And then rounds begins in which each participant speaks to the same prompt.

Session 8: Girl Rising

Objective: To broaden understanding of gender inequities in education across the globe.

In this session, participants will watch two segments of the Girl Rising film: *Ruksana and Wadley*. Girl Rising advocates for girls through storytelling. While watching these two segments, educators may consider how the film (and corresponding book) might be used within an interdisciplinary study for fourth- and fifth-grade social studies, geography, and math (population, percentages, statistics) and for possible service projects.

Recommended Protocol: "Consultancy Protocol." This protocol helps participants develop the capacity to see and describe dilemmas. The dilemma being explored can be about the girls in the film, or how to integrate their stories into existing curriculum. An ideal opportunity is to do both an exploration of the dilemmas faced by Ruksana and Wadley and the challenge to incorporate them into new learning.

Session 9: Learning Theories and Gender

Objective: To consider how new learning about gender and learning theories can be used to change practice and ensure growth in gender equity for students (may require two or three sessions depending on the length of time allotted for each session).

In this session, participants will read (or reread) theories of Abraham Maslow, Lev Vygotsky, and Benjamin Bloom. Participants will be asked to think about gender, gender bias, and gender health when reading through the theories and then write comments in the margins or in a notebook. These notes might include questions, connections, or requests for further reading.

Recommended Protocol: "Three Levels of Text Protocol." This protocol is designed to deepen the understanding of a text and explore implications for participants' work. The three levels are (1) literal—a participant reads a summary of the theory; (2) interpretation—states what he/she thinks about the passage (connections to current learning mission); and (3) implications—what implications does this theory, together with new learning, have on future actions in classroom practice or other interactions with students? Participants will either preread a theory by one of the educational theorists or be provided with time to read at the meeting.

These workshop sessions have mixed topic readings. Rather than running sessions focused on research that has interconnected concepts, you might instead decide to engage the entire staff in looking at all the relevant topics featured on your bubble chart. These might include Bias, Society/Culture, School Visual Culture, Behaviors and Language, Parents, and Curriculum.

Or you might decide to pair up some of those categories and have teams share out their research and findings. If possible, consider having everyone participate in all the new learning as second-hand accounting can fall short of participating in a full and enriching learning experience unless you have excellent communicators to report out.

A common occurrence in this type of new learning is when participants relate the new learning to a piece of literature, a video, or a personally relevant experience. Stopping a session to engage in an unplanned resource can distract from the learning at hand, but these connections should not be dismissed as they can very often enrich the experience. Setting up a shared folder, entitled "Connections" in which staff can place new reading, videos, and other connections will validate the contribution and ensure that potentially valuable information is not missed. The connections folder should be explored by teams during one of the learning sessions.

CHOOSING THE RIGHT LEADING TEAM

While it's meaningful to have everyone on board, the fact is that some people just won't be. There are those who are aware of gender-equity issues and the impact that gender bias will have for girls and boys in the future, but others may not understand why this topic is worthy of attention. Instead they may believe that girls and boys are different and any new contradictory information is not worth considering.

There are distinct differences between males and females but those differences are not grounds for inequitable treatment. A misunderstanding of the goals or lack of awareness about the issues at hand can cause meetings to go astray. Or, the committee may be comprised of good people without authority or those with authority but little vision. The ideal team will have everyone on board with the right staff members in the lead so that the mission is organized with a vision and a plan of action.

The people to drive change show enthusiasm and commitment, display trustworthiness, and structure meetings with agreed upon norms to minimize distraction and to stay on task. There are key characteristics and behaviors of those who can drive change. There are five essential skills to either look for or to help staff develop prior to creating a new initiative like a program to evaluate a school's gender health.[1]

1. Collaborative Intention—Individuals maintain an open and non-defensive presence.
2. Truthfulness—Creating a climate of openness to deal with difficult issues.
3. Self-Accountability—Finding solutions rather than someone to blame.

4. Self-Awareness and Awareness of Others—Seeking to understand oneself and others as well as the culture and context of circumstances.
5. Problem Solving and Negotiating—Using problem-solving methods to promote a cooperative rather than competitive atmosphere.

FORMING AN ACTION PLAN

A great deal of work should have been accomplished by this point. Staff members should have met, brainstormed, toured, and learned together. They've come to a new understanding of their own behaviors, student and parent behaviors, societal pressures, and biases that lead to gender inequity right within their own school buildings. Now it's time for action and change. It's time to for an action plan.

A good tool to use while developing an action plan is Mark Moore's Strategic Triangle. Moore is a professor at Harvard who promotes the idea of "public value." There are many personalized versions of the Strategic Triangle. The questions in Figure 4.3 are at the heart of what needs to be asked and answered during this school-wide or district-wide initiative on gender equity.

The first piece of the triangle is "Public Value." Those considering a gender-equity initiative see its value in improving lives. But does the public hold the same value? Are there stakeholders in your organization who may find this without value or even harmful? For success, a plan to educate and persuade may be the first step in the plan. Politics can be key in an unmandated initiative. Giving parents information about how a gender-equity initia-

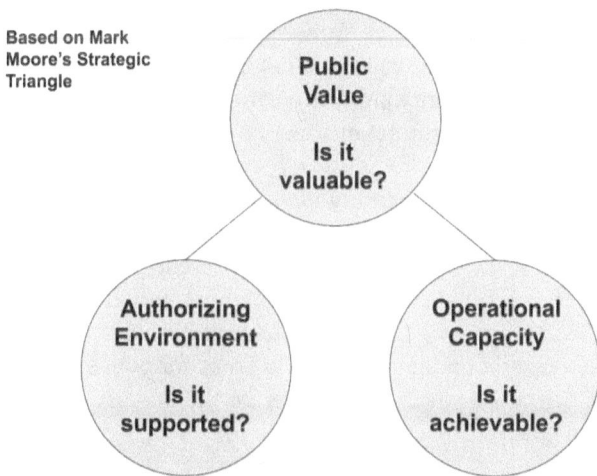

Figure 4.3. Bubble Chart Based on Mark Moore's Triangle

tive lifts both girls *and* boys can calm the fears of those who fear boys will be minimized. Through informed conversations, parents can learn that while gender inequity limits girls' opportunities, it can also box in boys with outdated and harmful definitions of what it means to be a successful male.

When thinking about the plan, consider who all the stakeholders are—parents, teachers, administrators, students—and how including them in the process will be developed and organized. Making a concerted effort to include parents across cultures will bring to light the need to respect cultures at the same time as enlightening parents to the benefits to children and the greater society when gender equity is respected.

The second triangle, "Authorizing Environment" prompts consideration of what needs to be done for plan approval. The authorizing environment can include colleagues, administrators, and parents once again. This time, however, the consideration is not on whether or not there is value in gender-equity education, but if there is a willingness to pursue and support it. A plan may sound like a fine idea in theory, but resistance can be met for any number of reasons.

It's important to know who is in the authorizing environment and to provide guidance and information needed to foster a willingness on their part to grant approval and enthusiasm. The final piece of the triangle is operational capacity. Does everyone involved have not only the materials they need, but also the time and energy to take part as a fully engaged participant? If there is not enough materials or ample time to ensure success, a plan will need to be created to provide those essential elements.

The action plan in Figure 4.4 is an expansion of an if/then statement developed at the beginning of the initiative to now show actionable items. It differs from the classroom action plan in chapter 3 in that this one adds key columns that are necessary when working with a larger group of parents and teachers. Also added to this plan is a column for potential barriers and for communication. Moving forward, the creation of a full rubric complete with principles and measurement actions can be included in the evaluation process.

The Strategic Action Plan in Figure 4.5 provides a different focus for the plan and provides for opportunities to consider equality and contributions in the action. Each of the organizers bring a different perspective and nuances on the goals. In the initial stages of development, utilizing as many organizers and thinking maps as possible will engage participants in new thinking and ultimately zero in on the most critical areas for both short and long-term plans. There can be one overarching plan for the initiative/program and subplans for team goals.

PARENTS AND GREATER COMMUNITY

During the tours and discussions, teachers may describe parents as the architects of gender bias and observe that students arrive at school with already well-defined attitudes about gender. There may be stories about gender-biased conversations during parent-teacher conferences. When teachers witness frequent examples of gender stereotyping among parents, they may not see a clear or politically correct path toward engaging parents in a gender-equity initiative. Teachers should be encouraged to use the new learning to engage parents in a gender-equity conversation and sharing the excitement of all the new learning that is taking place in the school on this topic, emphasizing the advantages to their children.

Just as careful selection of the school professionals for the Leading Team is critical, so too it is for the selection of parent participants as well. You might decide to include all or some parents from the very beginning of your initiative as part of your Leading Team or to bring them on during some point during the learning process. A parent learning team might be for parents alone with an educator as a facilitator or integrated right within your existing educator teams. Knowing your parent population is key to bringing these valuable stakeholders into the learning process.

There are a few ways to prepare parents and community members for conversations and initiatives on gender equity. Book clubs, parent information sessions on gender positive conversations at home or the impact of

Strategic Action Plan	Equal Opportunities	Valuing All Contributions	Sustaining Gender Equity
We will create an environment for all our students in which their rights, responsibilities and opportunities will not depend on whether or not they were born male or female.	Provide open access and encouragement to all students. Ensure that voices of all students are heard. Encourage students to pursue passions without gender bias limitations.	Assess classroom libraries and content area text for representation of all genders. Acknowledge students of all genders for their accomplishments across all academic areas and school activities.	Participate in ongoing gender equity professional development. Engage community members in gender equity learning. Continue monitoring visual culture in school buildings.

Figure 4.4. Strategic Action Plan Graphic

Creating a Gender Healthy School

Goal:
Results/Accomplishments:

Action Steps What Will Be Done?	Responsibilities Who Will Do It?	Timeline By When? (Day/Month)	Resources A. Resources Available B. Resources Needed	Potential Barriers A. What individuals or organizations might resist? B. How?	Communications Plan Who is included? What methods? How often?
Step 1:			A. B.	A. B.	
Step 2:			A. B.	A. B.	
Step 3:			A. B.	A. B.	

Evidence of Success (How will we know that we are making progress? What are our benchmarks?)
Evaluation Process (How will we determine that our goal has been reached? What are your measures?)

Figure 4.5. Creating a Gender-Healthy School

social media, and guest speakers who pursued nontraditional careers hold the potential to create a smooth pathway. Parents are a key part of the authorizing agents and public value segments of the strategic triangle. It is essential that this relationship is nurtured and that parents become engaged members of the process.

For some parents, the idea of gender equity is about favoring girls over boys. They may fear that boys will get short shrift in an environment that takes on a gender-equity initiative. It's important to keep in mind that while school staff has been actively engaged in the new learning, in many cases, the parents have not. Clear and positive communication is key.

The materials provided for staff workshop sessions may be considered for parents as well. Another valuable handout is Harvard's "For Families: 5 Tips for Preventing and Reducing Gender Bias."[2] Parents are the children's first and potentially best teacher. Supporting parents to promote more diverse concepts of gender may reduce stereotypes and create more gender-equitable communities in the future.

FACILITATING A MOVEMENT

Schools are the center of many communities and, as such, have the power and influence to not only change what happens inside the school, but what happens in the larger community. Part of the engagement involves consistent work over time. Consider the types of explicit and implicit bias that people face each and every day. Cosmetics commercials send messages of elusive beauty to women and strength and endurance to men. Students, too, are receiving similar gender-specific micromessages at home, at school, and in larger society.

Girls and boys continue to be targets of extreme social pressure through traditional media and social media outlets. Schools can decide if that is part of the outside world and not a school matter, or decide that schools are the perfect place to begin an ongoing process of addressing gender equity within and outside of the school. For schools taking such a proactive approach, there are ways to bring the entire community together in the quest for gender equity.

- Invite guest speakers that can include parents who have careers that defy gender stereotypes.
- Create a Community Book Club that includes books on gender equity.
- Develop a contest for local businesses that promote gender equity. For example, clothing stores that sell clothing without gender stereotypes or who advertise in gender respectful, rather than exploitative, ways.
- Hold a movie night with showings of films like "Redraw the Balance," "Creating Gender-Equity Schools," and segments of the "Girl Rising" film, along with discussion sessions that might include Q&As with educators and/or small breakout discussion sessions on specific areas covered in the films.
- Hold a movie night with showings of videos like Tony Porter's "A Call to Men" and a book study of select chapters of "The Boy Crisis" by Warren Farrell and John Gray.
- Social Media Detectives—Assign groups to watch music videos on YouTube (e.g., Taylor Swift's "You Need to Calm Down" or Cardi B and Bruno Mars's "Please Me"). Discuss the language and visual messages being sent to young girls and boys. Consider a plan to influence social media celebrities.
- Photo Contests—Community members submit photographs that represent to them the spirit of gender equity and equality.
- Writing Share—Community members submit writing to share at a gender equity gathering with gender as the central focus. This could be about their hopes for their own children or a reflection on how their own gender either afforded or denied them opportunities. It could be something as personal as the stories told on NPR's Moth Radio Hour or a Poetry Slam. Keeping it open to all styles encourages a sharing of not just a passion for gender equity but culture as well.
- Video Game Review—Ask boys and girls to review the characters in their favorite video game, with a focus on how the characters display gender

stereotypes and how that might influence students their age or students who are younger.

There is a great deal to consider when developing a full school plan to evaluate gender equity and then ultimately implementing the plan. Some of the graphics earlier in this chapter will help organize thoughts and opinions. The action plan such as the one in chapter 3 can be more fully developed to include elements that guide participants to consider varied responsibilities and potential barriers within the community.

Developing a full and robust gender-equity initiative that is school or district-wide is a challenging and meaningful undertaking. With a solid and inclusive plan, fully realized professional development workshops along with a committed team, schools can nurture an inclusive and equitable environment for all students and pave the way for future opportunities, free from gender limitations.

NOTES

1. James W. Tamm and Ronald J. Luyet, "Radical Collaboration: Five Essential Skills to Overcome Defensiveness and Build Successful Relationships," 2nd ed. (HarperBusiness, HarperCollins Publishers, 2004). https://www.amazon.com/Radical-Collaboration-Defensiveness-Successful-Relationships/dp/0060742518.

2. Alexis Ditkowsky, "For Families: 5 Tips for Preventing and Reducing Gender Bias," Making Caring Common, October 11, 2018, https://mcc.gse.harvard.edu/resources-for-families/5-tips-for-preventing-and-reducing-gender-bias.

Chapter Five

Introduction to Student Learning

Including students as an integral part of the learning process creates an opportunity for them to learn a new set of skills and gain a new perspective on gender equity. The following two chapters contain lessons that can be used as stand-alone lessons, integrated into current curriculum, or to serve as an inspiration to develop a full and robust elementary program tailored to the needs of a specific classroom or school building.

Before including students in the process of learning about gender and building a healthier environment, it's important that educators have done a fair amount of learning first. Fully exploring the research outlined in this book, from the preface through chapter 4, and creating professional development opportunities to strengthen teaching practice can build a strong foundation to begin teaching students.

Understanding at least some of the latest research on biological gender differences will enhance an educator's ability to notice if findings seem consistent with the behaviors and attitudes of their own students. Considering how gender expectations influence students present day and into their adulthood can put more proper weight on the need for sensitivity on the topic. This is more fully explored in chapter 9.

Sociologist Jeffrey J. Arnett, in describing the steps in human socialization, outlined three main goals. The first is that socialization teaches impulse control and helps people develop a conscience. This is considered to be done naturally as children and adults pick up on the expectations within their society and moderate their impulses. The second is that socialization teaches people how to live within certain roles such as professional, gender, and personal roles like parenthood and marriage. The third is that socialization develops shared meanings and value.[1]

Educators can elevate those goals to include teaching about gender, addressing the associated cultural expectations and supporting student growth by helping them see beyond perceived limitations. As educators witness each school day, socialization is not cultivated and then fixed. Rather, it is fluid. Impulse control can weaken when a child is paired with children with weaker boundaries and poorer socialization skills.

Children may enter school with a sense of self and then have it shift in school with exposure to different gender norms or pressures. There might be a shared meaning with a group outside of school and a completely different one within school. Children are faced with adult expectations of socialization and very different ones from their peers. As students grow throughout their elementary years, teachers who are mindful of gender issues can help students course correct as they move through phases of childhood.

The entire topic of gender and gender expectations can be both personal and political. As a result, many people try to avoid the topic altogether. Educators may worry about push back from parents and about entering a realm that feels uncomfortable. As detailed in chapter 1, even some neurobiologists prefer to avoid the subject completely because of how politically charged the topic can be. But lessons about gender equity need not be politically charged or unsettling.

Lessons about gender equity for children are built on ideas of kindness, fairness, and individuality. They quite simply include how all people can feel different, excluded, included, entitled, or limited because of gender. Teachers teach lessons about fair play and kindness on a regular basis. Incorporating an understanding and opening up conversations about gender can help support those lessons as they deal with real and substantive issues children face.

In many classrooms, there are students who feel uncertain about limitations because of their gender. A teacher who also understands intersectionality, the additional layers of bias experienced by some students, can support children by being mindful of individual needs. In considering which lessons to use in the next two chapters, also consider how modifying these lessons might add additional depth to the conversations students will have. Knowing students in the class and reflecting on the possible outcomes of lessons can guide teachers in deciding on lesson selection.

LESSONS AS EFFECTIVE PREVENTION AND INTERVENTIONS

Conversations about differences or conflict among students is often highly charged. Rather than "on the spot" interventions that are often associated with gender conflicts, intersectionality lessons can be preemptive and help prevent conflicts in the first place or serve as reference points when addressing students. At every school recess, there are countless conversations with boys on topics such as giving equal time at the ball court to the girls. Perhaps instead regular discussions about gender equality might strengthen socialization skills rather than fuel resentment over giving up what you want or need, such as being asked to sacrifice play time.

Socialization is more than just learning to compromise and playing nicely at recess. It is also an essential component of self-esteem. Picture the pain of a child not knowing how to deal with overwhelming emotions and being met by a much larger adult trying to get him to speak. Consider instead a lesson for the whole class so that expressing emotions is considered a strength instead of a weakness for girls and boys.

As emotions heighten and tensions rise, having a more neutral reference point of a past lesson can depersonalize a conflict. Instead of asking who did what to whom in an interpersonal struggle, referencing a lesson and those outcomes has the power to deescalate the situation and give time for reflection. A simple question about how their conflict is similar or different than the one they learned about in class can steer a student away from an angry stance to a more reflective one.

The value of gender-equity lessons is not just about controlling conflict. In fact, the lessons are about something much more powerful. They are about helping students see opportunities where they might have seen limits and are now able to express instead of swallow emotions. Where feelings of entitlement are present, gender-equity lessons might instead teach fairness. Gender lessons can move students from a state of confusion to a peaceful understanding.

The lessons in the next two chapters have grade-level recommendations that can serve as a guide. However, in looking through all the lessons, you might see that a lesson listed for another grade-level range is more appropriate for your class. While these lessons may be considered suitable for a wide range of ages, checking in with teachers in other grade levels to make sure they haven't already taught a lesson would avoid redundancy. Better yet, coordinating these lessons across classrooms and grade levels will ensure that students continue to be exposed to ideas of gender equity and that lessons are built one upon the other.

Thinking about your own students and issues you might like to address will help guide you to the appropriate lessons for your class. "How can I possibly fit this into a jam-packed day?" is a reasonable question. Consider incorporating some of the lessons into a writing class, as part of the morning routine, or within character education lessons. The lesson focused on the Equal Rights Amendment can be incorporated into a social studies unit, the Girl Rising lesson into a geography unit, and the Brain Science lesson into a science class.

Teachers are encouraged to use as many of these lessons as possible and to create their own lessons. New lessons can be created out of a new need identified or to utilize valuable resources available in individual schools. As students construct new understandings, a regular conversation or look back on lessons will help them develop more solid opinions and ideas. Differentiating lessons, just as teachers would do for math or writing curriculum, can add needed nuance. Writing additional scenarios that address the same theme but that address current school issues or classroom climate will strengthen the learning experience.

The goal for these lessons is not to change minds or tastes. If boys truly like superhero backpacks, they should be encouraged to embrace that choice. If a girl has absolutely no interest in soccer and likes to play with dolls, then her choice should be embraced. These lessons are not about blurring lines, but questioning who and why those lines were drawn in the first place. Some of the lessons are to provide food for thought, others to question whether their choices are truly their own, and others to emphasize ideas of fairness.

NOTE

1. J. Arnett, "Broad and Narrow Socialization: The Family in the Context of a Cultural Theory," *Journal of Marriage and the Family* 57, no. 3 (1995): 617.

Chapter Six

Primary Lessons for Students

Lesson: Backpack Walk
Grade Levels: Kindergarten, first, and second grades
Lesson Outcomes: Students will have the opportunity to learn that some choices seem to stem from gender norms and they will be encouraged to think about the thinking that supports these choices.
Materials Needed: Students' backpacks
Time Required: Thirty-five to forty minutes
Methods: Students will use their own and classmates' backpack choices as a means of discussion and evaluation.

   1. *Backpack Predictions:* Bring all the students' backpacks into the classroom and put them in a pile so students can see each one. Ask them not to say which one is theirs. Tell students that today they are going to participate in a prediction experiment. Their job is to tell whether a backpack belongs to a girl or to a boy.

- Hold each backpack up and ask students to raise their hands if they believe this belongs to a boy. Then ask students to raise their hands if they believe it belongs to a girl.
- By a show of majority of hands raised, place the backpacks in a row marked girls and a row marked boys.
- When all backpacks have been placed, ask students to stand next to their backpack.
- Ask students to talk about what they are observing. If prompts are needed, consider asking: How did we do at predicting the girls' and boys' backpacks? Will you please share what you are noticing/seeing? Why do you think you are seeing these differences? How do you feel about seeing

these differences? Why do you think that the girls and boys have such different tastes? Write down comments that would prompt further thought.

2. *Backpack Talk:* Use backpacks as a means of conversation in small groups or one to one.

- With backpacks in their lap, ask students to describe the purpose of the backpack. Write down responses on chart board or board.
- Ask students to describe what design is on their backpack. If it's a superhero or a princess, ask students if they or a parent chose the backpack, if they would like to be a superhero or princess and what that means to them.
- As they provide answers, take notes about what they are saying and their demeanor as this information tells you more about students' thinking that may be useful in informing future conversations.
- Go back to the original question about what the purpose of a backpack is. Then ask students, "If this is just something to carry our lunches and books in, then why are all these decorations on them?"

Depending on the age and developmental readiness of the class, this lesson may just be to bring awareness or can be further developed into a discussion and activities around identifying which images are gender based. See intermediate lesson, "Images and Your Brain" to expand.

3. *Backpack Trade:* Tell students that there will be a "temporary" backpack trade today. Assure them they will get their own backpack returned right after the activity!

- Ask students to bring their backpacks into the classroom and place on their desks or tables.
- Give students a few minutes to take a walk around the classroom to think about some backpacks they might like to have in a temporary trade.
- Choose a name from the hat and ask that student to make a backpack trade.
- When that student has chosen, he/she can then choose the next name from the hat. Continue this until all students have made a trade.
- Now it's time for feedback. Ask students to explain why they made the trade. What was it about their new backpack that they liked? Was it similar to their own or very different? If it was different, what was it about the difference that they liked and inspired them to make the trade? If it was similar, ask the student to describe what it is about that style that appeals to them?

In whatever activity the classroom teacher opts to do with students, the emphasis should be on helping students think about their choices and whether they are based on free choice or if the choice is colored by how they feel about gender and fear about not affiliating closely enough with social constructs of gender.

Follow-Up Assignments: There are a few closing or follow-up activities that students can choose from:

- In small groups, students create videos to advertise backpacks that would appeal to all children.
- Students write persuasive letters to classmates about new or existing opinion on backpacks, their usefulness, and their designs.
- Independently or in small groups, students design a new backpack that has improvements over the one they brought to school. These improvements can include anything, with an emphasis on an improved design.

Lesson: How Would You Feel? What Would You Do?
Grade Levels: Kindergarten, first, and second grades
Lesson Outcomes: Students will be able to understand the emotions behind hurt feelings of both girls *and* boys and think about ways to express those emotions.
Materials Needed: Scenarios printed out on half sheet of paper with questions on bottom half. Writing paper or notebooks to record responses.
Time Required: Thirty-five to forty minutes
Methods: Students will use real-life scenarios to work through solutions to gender-based problems and limitations.

- For nonreaders or early readers, read through these scenarios one at a time with a whole class or in small groups (if enough adults are available for small groups).
- For readers, encourage them to read together and then to discuss their thoughts and opinions. To differentiate, encourage students to write their thoughts down if they process better through the written word.

The scenarios can be displayed on a projection screen as well. Students read the scenarios and either independently or in small groups answer the questions.
Alternate Method: Teacher video records the scenarios and uploads them to a shared folder. With this method, students can watch the video more than once which may facilitate more thoughtful responses.

Scenario 1: Jake and Carla are at recess and kicking a ball to each other. Jake's friend Mark runs up to them and says to Jake, "Come on play ball with us. Why are you talking to a girl?" Jake isn't sure what to do. He doesn't want the boys to think he likes girls, but Carla is his friend and they were having a good time. Jake's face turns red. He looks at Carla and then runs off to play with the boys.

- How was Jake feeling?
- How was Carla feeling?
- Could Jake or Carla have done something different? If so, what could he or she have done?

Note: You can put this scenario in worksheet format with ample room for responses.

Scenario 2: Kenny was playing with his friends before school. His shoelace became loose and he tripped as he was running. As he landed on the ground, he felt a burning pain in his knee. Kenny didn't cry because he would have been embarrassed. He just held on to his knee and didn't look up at any of his friends who were asking if he was okay.

- Why do you think Kenny held back his tears?
- Do you think it's right that Kenny held back his tears?
- How did holding back his tears make Kenny feel?
- What could Kenny's friends do to help him?
- Would it have been easier for Kenny to cry if he was a girl?

Scenario 3: Robert's mother and father are lawyers. They have both been working the same amount of time for the same company. Robert's mother makes less than Robert's father. Please discuss why you think Robert's mother makes less money.

In the three scenarios, encourage students to say their true feelings, to make sure they are listening and not judging what someone else says. Tell students that the whole point of this activity is to hear and take note of classmate's thoughts and ideas. If possible, give students an audio recorder so they can tape themselves or use a program such as Flipgrid or Google Recorder if students are old enough to operate these types of programs and platforms.

Lesson: It's A Girl Thing/It's A Boy Thing
Lesson Outcomes: Students will broaden their understanding of activities beyond things girls like to do vs. things boys like to do. Students will gain a greater appreciation for the commonalities among boys and girls.

Grade Levels: Kindergarten, first, and second grades
Time Required: Thirty-five to forty minutes
Materials Needed: Interactive whiteboard, chalkboard, or chart paper; sticky notes, pencils
Methods: Students will determine which activities and sports are "girl things" and which are "boy things." There are two different ways to conduct the activity.

1. Teacher creates a two-column chart on interactive whiteboard screen or chart paper. The header for the first column is GIRLS and the second column is BOYS. The teacher reads aloud an activity and asks students which activities should go in each column. The teacher records their answers in each column based on majority opinion.
2. Teacher lists a wide variety of different activities on the board on large Post-its, sentence strips, or large paper with magnetic backing. The teacher asks for volunteers to move each activity to its proper place under GIRLS or BOYS. This can also be easily produced for a smart-board type of projector so students could drag the activity as well.

- When the placement of each activity is complete, ask students to come to the board in small groups to look over the list again.
- When they've all completed this look, ask students if these all seem right or if it's possible that some of these activities actually belong in both columns.
- Ask the students if they like to do activities that appear in both columns.
- Open up discussion about why so many activities are thought to be for girls or boys but not both.
- Create a column entitled "Both Genders" or "People," and either ask for volunteers to move any sticky note or strip that they think should be moved, or discuss as a whole group and either the teacher or volunteers move the sticky notes to appropriate columns.
- Ask for volunteers to talk about what happened to the activities list as the class went on.
- Prompt students to describe if they agreed what was happening or if they had a different opinion about what should have happened.
- In small groups, ask students to discuss what they learned from this activity.
- *Optional:* Instruct students to write a few sentences or paragraph on the learning outcomes of the class.

Ideas for activities: Soccer, violin, board games, dolls, hiking, video games, chess, football, baseball, basketball, tennis, running, reading, experimenting, studying, singing, acting, watching TV, painting or drawing, and writing.

Challenge: Try one activity you listed as something the other gender likes to do. Describe how it felt to do this new activity.

Lesson: Election Time!
Lesson Outcomes: Students will identify gender as a possible factor in selecting candidates for office.
Grade Levels: Kindergarten, first, and second grades
Materials Needed: Campaign posters, pencils, tally chart, voting slip (sticky notes)
Optional: Voting booth, hat.
Time Required: Thirty to thirty-five minutes
Methods: Students vote for either a male or female candidate for president.

- Create very similar campaign promises, with only slight differences. For example, one might say, "I'll make sure everything is fair" and the other might say, "Everyone will be treated the same." The primary difference between the two candidates is that one is a girl and the other is a boy.
- Either create a voting booth or collect votes in a fun hat.
- Hand students sticky notes or voting slips and instruct them to write their choice on the paper provided.
- Calculate the results and display. This can be done by asking for a volunteer to record the tallies or using a base ten display on the interactive smartboard so that each student can come to the board to move a piece to the boy or girl column.
- Ask students to volunteer to share who they voted for and why. If the results show that the boy candidate won, probe further by asking why the students favored the boy over the girl. Other questions can lead to a lively and thought-provoking conversation:

  - What is it about your candidate that you liked better than the other one?
  - Is the boy candidate more qualified than the girl? How do you know that?
  - If you were running for an office, how fair do you think it would be if kids voted for you only because you were a boy or a girl?

Extension Activity: Have students create posters for a candidate that describes qualities that are important.

Lesson: Lego Challenge
Grade Levels: Kindergarten, first, second, and third grades
Objective: Students will develop a new understanding of beauty and function through the evaluation of newly constructed Lego creations.

Note: This lesson is most effective after an initial lesson in which students are able to initially identify that gender bias exists.
Materials Needed: Lego bricks, drawing paper, evaluation worksheet
Time Required: Two classes, thirty to forty-five minutes
Methods and Notes: Students will work in small groups of same gender to build Lego towers that either serve a purpose or display a beautiful design. The reason they are working in same gender groups is so that they can evaluate (1) if there is a difference in how the girls or boys designed the tower and (2) to appreciate the skill and beauty in each one, regardless of assumptions about gender. They will then evaluate each other's designs and discuss outcomes. Groups should have privacy shields up so their sketches and final project is hidden from view. When the projects are done and before evaluation, move them to a different place in the room to ensure that students are not aware of who built which Lego creation.

Day 1:

- Tell students the day before the class that they will work with a group to design a Lego tower and that you would like them to brainstorm ideas about what they would like to build. The tower can either be built for beauty or function. Explain to them the difference between beauty (design, like a sculpture) and function (serves a "practical" purpose).
- Tell students that you'd like them to first decide with their group (keeping the groups the same gender) if it is for design or function. Examples of functions could be a building, garden, car, or a new something that serves a practical purpose.
- Give students sketch paper or computers to draw and write down their ideas and to make sure that everyone's name is on the sketch.
- Encourage students to make sure everyone has contributed ideas and that they've reached a consensus. If they are having trouble, they should ask for assistance.

Day 2:

- Instruct the students to gather in their groups from yesterday. Either hand back their sketches, or tell them to login to the computer to access their work there.
- Show students where they will be working and where to find their supply of Legos if it is not easily accessible.
- Provide students with ample time to construct their Lego tower.
- Explain to students that their job now is to jot notes (evaluate) while looking at another group's Lego Tower design. Hand students one evaluation sheet per group and instruct them to come to an agreement on what to

circle and write. See Figure 6.1 for an example of an evaluation sheet. For younger students, review word meanings prior to evaluation.
- When all groups have completed their evaluation sheets, they can present their findings to the rest of the class. A fun way to do this is to have the class walk from tower to tower as the audience while the evaluation group is presenting. After all the students have completed their evaluation presentations, some additional teacher questions will bring the purpose of the class into view.

  - Teacher might say: I love the careful evaluations you did that show how each piece of work is unique. Some work is towering, tall and sturdy. Others are smaller, detailed and elegant. I'm seeing such great value in all of these pieces of work. I have one last assignment for you. By looking at your evaluation sheet or getting up and taking a look at your classmates' work again, can you find one thing in their work that you would use in yours next time? If so, what would that be?
  - After giving students ample time, getting their feedback and writing down some of their answers, ask students: Would it matter if what you learned or wanted to use in your work next time was done by a girl or a boy? Why/Why not? Please explain how looking at each other's work with the worksheet made a difference in your evaluations. In what ways would your evaluation have been different if you knew the gender of the students building it? What are some of your conclusions about learning from each other?

Lesson: A Boy Is . . . A Girl Is . . . Writing Activity
Lesson Outcomes: Students will describe the characteristics of boys and girls
Grade Levels: Kindergarten, first, and second grades
Materials Needed: Character traits chart (provide an age appropriate one!)
Time Required: Thirty-five to forty minutes
Methods: Students will determine if character traits seem more like they belong to boys or to girls by circling words on a character trait chart.

- Tell students that today their help is needed in figuring out what the characteristics are of boys and girls.
- Review a character traits chart and discuss if students need a refresher on what a character trait is.
- Give each student a character trait chart and a green and an orange marker. Tell students that they will circle a character trait word that seems like it belongs to a girl in green and a character trait that seems like it belongs to a boy in orange. Ask them to circle at least five words in green and five words in orange.

Lego Tower Challenge!

Names of students: (Evaluators)

_____

_____

Circle at least 2 words that describe the tower

awesome	beautiful	elegant
tall	colorful	creative
powerful	graceful	small
huge	pretty	useful

Other descriptive words:

_____

Figure 6.1. Lego Tower Challenge

- As students complete their work, give them a piece of tape and ask them to hang it somewhere in the classroom.
- Now, it's time for students to walk around the room and look at each other's responses. Instruct students that what they are looking for are any surprises, like a character trait for a boy that seemed like a girl or vice versa. When they are finished, they may return to their seats.
- In a whole class discussion, ask students if there were any surprises on the character trait charts they were looking at.
- If the teacher sees a pattern, (and this is likely to happen) such as boys are consistently identified as brave or fearless or girls are consistently identified as loving or kind, then the teacher can open up a discussion by asking if this is always true and why students believe this to be true.

Lesson: Color Me Beautiful
Lesson Outcomes: Students will be able to appreciate differences and consider qualities they had not previously seen.
Grade Levels: Kindergarten, first, and second grades
Time Required: Thirty-five to forty minutes

Materials: Small strips of different colored paper, container to hold the strips (hat, basket), and chart paper and interactive whiteboard for recording responses.

Methods: Students will use strips of colored paper to think about what makes a color beautiful.

- Teacher cuts small strips of colored paper and puts them into a container such as a hat or basket.
- Passing around the basket, teacher asks students without looking to reach into the container and take a strip of paper.
- After all students have their strip, students are given a color qualities chart like the one in Figure 6.2.
- Students are then asked to write some good qualities about the color on the chart. For example, many pretty flowers are purple or black is the color of the night sky. Or maybe their qualities will be simple, with one-word descriptions like "cheerful."
- Students are assured that picking out a color that is not their favorite is also a good thing because "part of what we are doing today is finding good qualities we may not have seen before."
- Walk around classroom, asking students about their responses, encouraging those who may be struggling with the assignment.
- When all students have completed the assignment, ask for volunteers to show on the projector camera, or to write on chart paper or a whiteboard or blackboard.
- Teacher now poses questions and prompts discussion so that the learning objectives become clear. Some questions might include: "How did you feel about this assignment?" "Who got a color they didn't like? Did you learn anything good about that color? Tell us what you see now."
- At the end of the class, teacher wraps up by conveying this message in his/her own words or in these words: "Sometimes we like or don't like things because of what our siblings or friends think. But part of growing up and being an interesting and caring person is being able to see good qualities in things and people if we just spend a little time believing those good things are there. I always used to say I didn't like orange, but then I realized I just don't like to wear orange, but that orange is beautiful like the sun and my favorite fruit."

Note: This is a good foundational lesson to reference when children are having difficulty with each other because of differences in gender, color, or behavior.

Lesson: Gender Musical Chairs

Color Quality List

Beautiful	Cheerful
Sad	Powerful
Bold	Awesome
Happy	Sunny
Loud	Muddy
Pale	Dark
Calm	Fresh
Jazzy	Bright

Figure 6.2. Color Quality List Worksheet

Note: A good alternate method for this lesson is to have older students in grades three to five model this with kindergarten to second-grade students as audience members. While fun for some children, teachers may consider if this lesson will trigger anxiety in some young children. This can also be another opportunity to build community among younger and older students.
Lesson Outcomes: Students will learn about providing equitable opportunities for everyone.
Grade Levels: Kindergarten, first, and second grades
Time Required: Thirty-five to forty minutes
Materials: Colored index cards (blue, pink or purple, green or other pairing) chairs, music
Methods: Students will play musical chairs with a gender twist.

- Set out enough chairs for students, minus one, per usual musical chairs setup. For a refresher on the rules, doing an internet search on "how to play musical chairs" will yield many results.
- Tape a colored index card onto each chair. One color will represent boys and the other color girls. The cards might even be labeled with the word "girl" or "boy."

- Calculate how many girl and boy cards to put on chairs. The goal is to make it unequal so that girls or boys are "out" not only because they didn't reach a seat when the music stopped, but because they didn't reach a seat that was marked for their gender when the music stopped. (Example: If the class has eight girls and you want the girls to be out, then make fewer than eight girl cards.)
- When the game has been completed, ask students how they felt about this game. These questions can include: "What do you think of the usual way you have played musical chairs in the past?" "In what ways was this one different?" "How did that make you feel?" The answers to these questions will no doubt prompt comments about unfairness and that it shouldn't matter if you are a boy or a girl, you should be able to sit.

Lesson: Brain Science
Lesson Outcomes: Students will understand that our brains work differently and can grow and develop because of actions people take.
Grade Levels: Kindergarten, first, and second grades
Time Required: Thirty minutes
Materials: Model of a brain or a projected model from a photo that shows various angles of the brain.
Methods: Students will learn through direct instruction and modeling of the brain about how it changes and grows.

- Gather students in a circle to tell them that today they will learn a little bit about the brain. Tell students that as they get older they will learn more about all the different parts of the brain (pointing to the different brain segments), what they are called, and what they do. But for today, we are going to see what it looks like and learn about what the brain does.
- If a model is available, pass it around so the students can touch it, comment, or ask questions. If it's on a projector, students can be invited to come up to the screen to look.
- Ask students what they think the brain does and discuss answers. They are likely to have different ways to say it helps us think.
- Tell students that the brain helps us do so much more than just think. It controls our breathing and movement and just about everything else in our bodies! The brain is incredibly important.
- Let students know that scientists are studying the brain and they have found out two things so far: (1) The brain of males (boys) and females (girls) are different. Parts of their brains actually work differently too! "Isn't that so interesting?" But both brains are just as valuable. (2) The brain can actually change. So for example, if today you feel that you aren't as good as you'd like to be at building a house with Legos, or reading is a

little frustrating, or you have trouble thinking and talking about your feelings, that can all change! Many neuroscientists (people who study the brain) have seen parts of the brain thicken and change after people have practiced over and over again.
- Ask students to either write down one thing they would like to get better at or for early writers, they can ask someone to write it for them. If students have trouble thinking of something, an adult in the room can prompt thinking based on past experience with the student.
- When students have completed their thinking and writing about something they would like to get better at, ask them if they think it's possible they can get better, why that's possible, and what they can do to help their brains help them.

Note: This lesson has a simple premise and lays the foundation for future interventions with children. The boy who has trouble sharing his feelings, the girl who thinks she can't succeed in math, or children who feel unsuccessful at many things can have hope knowing that practice will more than likely help them grow a skill or share an emotion that was previously so difficult.

Extension Activity: Provide students with a printed outline of the brain to color and to write positive statements about the brain. Examples include: "My brain is growing!" "Our brains are different and special!"

Chapter Seven

Intermediary Lessons for Students

Lesson: Nontraditional Careers
Learning Outcomes: Students will understand how implicit biases play a role in the formation of their opinions about gender and careers.
Grade Levels: Third, fourth, fifth, and sixth grades
Time Required: Two days, thirty to forty minutes each day
Materials: Notepaper, career descriptions
Methods: Students will construct their own gendered image of a person in a career and expand their thinking about nontraditional careers.

Day 1:

- Select specific careers and write them on the board. These careers should include traditional male careers and female careers. They may include firefighter, pilot, nurse, teacher, doctor, computer engineer, and ballet dancer.
- Tell students that you'd like them to select one of those careers and draw a person who is doing that job and then name them. They may draw just the face or the entire body. In assigning a name, it is more likely that the gender will be obvious to classmates. (If it isn't, they can ask their classmate.)
- After everyone has completed their drawing, hang them throughout the classroom and have students do a walk to see all the drawings. They should take note paper to jot down anything that may come to mind. (Note: Instruct students that the quality of the artistic talent is not a consideration.)
- Assign groups of students to tally how many males and how many females were drawn for each profession.

- Discuss the outcomes by posing questions: "Why do you think so many of us thought of firefighters as men?" "Could a ballet dancer be a man?" "What are some of the reasons that men and women gravitate to one career more than another?"
- As students respond, record their answers on the board or electronic whiteboard.
- Review all the answers and congratulate students on insightful thoughts and then ask them if they think the way things are now have to continue to be that way in the future. If not, what can change?

Day 2: Students will select a career from the nontraditional careers list like the one below. Tell students that today you would like them to look over the nontraditional careers list and to complete one of the following assignments.

- Choose a nontraditional career that you believe you might like to try. What is it about this career that might appeal to you? What type of education will you need to excel at this work? What is the average salary for this job? Do you think there is any social stigma associated with someone of your gender doing this type of work? (Will people think you should not do this job?) Why do you think that is?
- Create a commercial advertising for people to enter nontraditional careers. What will you use to "sell people" on the idea to enter a nontraditional career? Using your best persuasive essay techniques, write an ad for the internet, TV, or newspaper that will include work, working conditions, appeal of the job, salary, and why people of your gender should consider this work.

Here are some nontraditional careers for women:

1. *Car mechanic:* Mechanics work on vehicles and take care of maintenance, such as adding fluids, replacing rotors, and repairing and replacing parts that have been damaged.
2. *Electrician:* Electricians are responsible for installing, maintaining, and repairing power systems and lighting.
3. *Firefighter:* Firefighters can be either volunteers or paid employees of towns and cities. Firefighters respond to emergencies, including extinguishing fires and assisting in car accidents.
4. *Engineer:* Being an engineer can include anything from mechanical engineering to civil engineering. Daily duties might include researching, creating, and evaluating complex systems in a variety of types of companies or government agencies.
5. *Computer technician:* Computer technicians can work as developers and programmers for small or large businesses.

6. *Chief executive officer:* A chief executive officer (CEO) is the highest-ranking executive in a company. Primary responsibilities include making major corporate decisions and managing the overall operations and resources of a company.
7. *Heavy equipment operator:* Heavy equipment operators use machines like bulldozers and backhoes to move materials and clear out sites for building.

Here are some nontraditional careers for men:

1. *Early education teachers:* Kindergarten and preschool teachers are responsible for teaching children ages eighteen months to six years old. They are also often responsible for the physical and emotional needs of children in this age group.
2. *Dental assistant:* Dental assistants examine and prepare patients for exams and other dental procedures.
3. *Occupational therapist:* Occupational therapists develop and implement treatment plans for patients who need help with daily living skills.
4. *Registered nurse:* Nurses provide the majority of the patient care during hospital stays and are responsible for treating patients and working with doctors on providing care.
5. *Ballet dancer:* Ballet dancers work with choreographers and other dancers to learn ballet dances, rehearse their roles, and perform in front of large audiences.
6. *Social worker:* Social workers focus on working with at-risk populations to ensure that their needs are being met. This might include senior citizens, children, or people living in poverty.

Lesson: The Feeling Game
Learning Outcomes: Students will learn the complexities of feelings and the challenges in determining emotions through only one means of observation.
Grade Levels: Third, fourth, fifth, and sixth grades
Time Required: Thirty-five to forty-five minutes
Materials: Photos of girls and boys with different facial expressions
Methods: Students will use observation skills and thoughtful discussion to deepen their understanding of initial perceptions about emotion.
Note: This lesson might be best facilitated with a school psychologist or social worker but can certainly be implemented by a teacher alone.

- Find a series of photos of girls and boys with different expressions. There are a wide range of them to be found in images on the internet. Print them

out large enough for the class to see or display them on a projector. Some emotions will be obvious: excited, surprised, and sad. But others should be more vague. There are a wide range of pleasant to unpleasant emotions, which include contempt, anger, heartbreak, fear, disgust, joy, happiness, amusement, jealousy, guilt, and shame.
- Ask students to volunteer to talk about what they think is the emotional state of the person in each photo. As an alternative, number the photos and have students write the number and related emotion on a paper before having the whole class discussion.
- As the students answer, prompt deeper thinking with questions such as "Is it possible that he is hurt rather than angry?" "Why would someone say they are hurt rather than angry?" "Do you think it's easier for girls to express hurt than it is for boys?" "If so, why do you think that is true?" "Is it possible to make mistakes when we think about how someone is feeling?" "What is the best way to know how someone is feeling?" "How can we have a conversation with someone about how they are feeling/their emotions?"

The teacher can guide students' conversations so that they can understand that talking about emotions is a skill like many other skills. Sometimes, understanding the emotional state of the other gender can be more challenging because our unique biology can create certain differences in us. The goal is to have differences complement and not cause conflict. The answer to that is talking about emotions and how that can look different for each of us and talking about emotions is one of the ways to become a healthy and whole person.

Lesson: How Would You Feel? What Would You Do?
Learning Outcomes: Students will be able to understand the emotions behind hurt feelings of both girls *and* boys and think about ways to express those emotions.
Grade Levels: Third, fourth, fifth, and sixth grades (Note: This lesson is also listed for kindergarten to second grade with different scenarios.)
Materials Needed: Scenarios printed out on half sheet of paper with questions on bottom half. Writing paper or notebooks to record responses. Optional: Flipgrid, Google Recorder
Time Required: Thirty-five to forty minutes
Methods: Students will collaborate to address peer-related social issues.
Alternate Method: Teacher video records the scenarios and uploads them to a shared folder. With this method, students can watch the video more than once, which may facilitate more thoughtful responses.

1. *Scenario 1:* Harry and Emily were giving a presentation to the class on their social studies project that they completed together. Although they had carefully planned their speaking parts, Harry frequently talked over Emily, interrupting her presentation, causing her to get confused about what she was going to say next. Emily told a friend that she was really tired of Harry doing very little of the hard work to prepare and then talking through the presentation as if he had done all the work.

   - What emotion or emotions do you think Emily was feeling during the presentation?
   - Do you think that the fact that Harry is a boy and Emily is a girl has anything to do with the obvious dynamic between the two students? If so, explain.
   - What are some of the ways that Emily could have prevented this type of interaction or ways to follow-up after the presentation?

2. *Scenario 2:* Kendrick arrives in school each morning, seeming rushed and in a bad mood. He often pushes past students to hang up his coat and backpack. When his classmates tell him to stop pushing, he grumbles and says something rude like "Stay out of my way." Kendrick doesn't really participate in class either. Kids have started to think he's weird and avoid him, which is making his behavior worse.

   - Could Kendrick's gender have something to do with his behavior? If so, in what ways do you think this might be contributing?
   - If there is anything that a classmate could do to help, what types of things might be worth trying to help Kendrick in finding happier ways to behave in school?

3. *Scenario 3:* At the end-of-the-year fifth-grade dance, most girls wore dresses and heels and fixed their hair in special ways. Two girls, Kelsey and Charisse, chose not to dress differently for the dance. Instead, they wore pants and flat shoes and kept their hair off their faces with hair ties. When they arrived at school, the girls were met with stares from the other girls. Some even asked if they forgot their dresses back in their closets.

   - What dress requirements do you think girls should have when attending a dance?
   - How do you think Kelsey and Charisse feel about the way they were treated by their classmates at the dance? Describe some of the feelings they might have had.

- What could other students in the class do to help Kelsey and Charisse feel better without causing even more embarrassment?

Note: In the three scenarios, encourage students to say their true feelings, to make sure they are listening and not judging what someone else says. Tell students that the focus of this activity is to hear and take note of classmates' thoughts and ideas. If possible, give students an audio recorder so they can tape themselves, or use a program such as Flipgrid or Google Recorder if students are old enough to operate programs and platforms like this.

Lesson: Girl Rising
Learning Outcomes: Students will identify the disparity between treatment of girls and boys in parts of the world and compare it to what takes place at home.
Grade Levels: Fifth and sixth grades
Time Required: Forty to forty-five minutes per session
Materials: Girl Rising film (segments available online, full video on Amazon Prime), compare/contrast graphic organizer, and world map. Optional: *Girl Rising* book.
Methods: Students will compare and contrast their lives to the lives of those depicted in *Girl Rising*. Extension activity may include social justice action plan.
Background Information: There are many organizations that support the life and education of girls across the world. Girl Rising does so through storytelling. By focusing on the lives of girls in need, the impact of bias against girls becomes real and impactful. They began with a film about nine girls and their communities that was translated into thirty different languages.

The following are key pieces of information when studying the education of girls worldwide: Girls who get a quality education are more likely to be healthier and better prepared to enter and succeed in the workforce. Education can give girls more opportunities to advocate for their own rights, contribute to their families and communities, and grow local and global economies. But over 130 million girls didn't go to school each day. Because of this, in 2017, nearly half a billion women worldwide still cannot read.

Day 1:

- Preview full movie to select which segments to show. *Wadley and Ruksana* may be age appropriate for fifth grade. Their ages are within range of fifth grade, and the subject matter is within the grasp of understanding.
- Provide an overview for students on the Girl Rising organization and what they do, that they tell girls' stories so that the statistics about girls and their

lack of education around the world come to life. "Today, we are going to see one of those stories. The story is about Wadley who lives in Haiti."
- Show students Haiti on the map or ask them to find Haiti on a world map if they have their own map. Ask students, "Considering their proximity to the equator and to water, what are some of the challenges that you think Wadley might face in her life?" Take responses from students and discuss.
- Show the video and encourage students to jot down any questions or comments they may have during the showing.
- Using a compare/contrast organizer, students list the ways their education is similar and different to Wadley's.

Days 2 and 3:

- Review the statistics on girls' education. "Today, we are going to see another girl's story. Her name is Suma and she lives in Nepal." Show students Nepal on the world map or ask them to find it on their own if they have their own map. To incorporate map skills into this lesson, consider asking them to identify bordering countries and predict the climate in Nepal based on its proximity to the equator.
- Show the video and encourage students to jot down any questions or comments they may have during the showing.
- Students will learn about Kamlari, a system practiced in Far-West Nepal, in which girl children of certain families have to work at employers' houses from their childhood. It is transferred from one generation to another. Although it is now outlawed, some children are returning to these families because they have no other source of income. Kamlari is bonded labor.

Students should brainstorm on ways they might help girls like Suma and Wadley get the education they deserve so that they can reach their full potential.

Extension Activities: Students can create a fundraiser in school to raise money for organizations like Girl Rising, Save the Children, or UNESCO.

Lesson: Virtual Tours and Conversations
https://education.microsoft.com/skype-in-the-classroom/find-guest-speakers
Learning Outcomes: Students will have the opportunity to learn from professionals in various fields and consider the role gender might or might not play in selection of a career.
Grade Levels: Third, fourth, fifth, and sixth grades
Materials Needed: Teacher Microsoft/Skype account, project/smartboard, and speakers

Time Required: Thirty-five to forty minutes
Methods: Utilizing Microsoft/Skype account, teacher will find opportunities for students to Skype with professionals in a variety of fields. This can include specifically seeking out women in nontraditional careers as field guides. Students will have the opportunity to pose questions to women about their professional goals and specifics about their area of work. Through Skyping, students may also reach out to students in other countries to gain a greater understanding of life as a boy or girl in countries across the world.

- Utilizing Microsoft/Skype account, teacher will look for guest speakers in a field that is related to a current field of study, being mindful to seek out women or men in nontraditional careers so that girls and boys will have a wider view of people in professional positions.
- In virtual field trips, students may take tours of businesses, environmental centers, museums, and energy farms across the world. Field trips rotate and new ones are frequently added. Teachers can seek out opportunities that will expand students' understanding of men and women in the workplace.

Lesson: Who Is Representing You?
Learning Outcomes: Students will learn about the gender distribution in government representation and consider if it needs to be brought into a better balance.
Grade Levels: Fourth and fifth grades
Time Required: Forty to forty-five minutes
Materials: Research material, notebooks, graphic organizers (congressional seats)
Methods: Students will either learn for the first time or refresh their memories about the United States Senate. Then, they will research how many men and how many women are in the United States Senate.

1. After students have had some time to read about the responsibilities of the United States Senate they will discuss the importance of the role of senators and how their decisions impact people's lives.
2. Students will then color in the US Senate seating chart in Figure 7.1. They will choose a color for men and a different color for women, making sure they indicate each color in the key at the bottom.
3. Looking at their chart, students should then answer the following questions, either by writing down their answers or small group/whole class discussion.

    - What is your chart showing?

- Why do you think these numbers look this way?
- Considering what we know about the responsibilities of a United States Senator, what do you think this will mean for men and for women in America and their particular interests?
- What are some ways that you think this could be changed in the future? Is there anything *you* could do to make changes?

Extension Activities: Assign students to research the history of the United States Senate and create a table showing the changes in gender representation over the past three elections. They will review the changes and do a presentation that presents the data along with speculation about why changes occurred.

Lesson: An Equal Rights Amendment
Lesson Outcomes: Students will learn about the history of the Equal Rights Amendment and consider how the efforts to get it passed impacted the rights of women.
Grade Levels: Fourth, fifth, and sixth grades
Time Required: Forty to forty-five minutes

Color the Senate!

Each circle represents one senate seat. (100 in total!)

Choose a color for female senators and another color for male senators, then color in the circles.

Key:
Female Senators: ○
Male Senators: ○

Figure 7.1.   Color the Senate

Materials: "A History of the Equal Rights Amendment" reading, ERA timeline

Methods: Students will consider why those who proposed the ERA thought this was necessary and what the history of this amendment proposal has meant for the progress of girls and women in society.

Day 1:

- Students will read the passage, "A History of the Equal Rights Amendment" in Figure 7.2.
- Then, students will create a timeline like the one in Figure 7.3 and complete it with key events, including the current year, indicating whether or not the Equal Rights Amendment passed. Students can do individual timelines or one large timeline to hang on a bulletin board along with the reading passage. This can be considered an appropriate sharing at any time of the year and particularly during March, which is Women's History Month.

Day 2:

- Students choose another amendment to the constitution, working in small groups. They can create another timeline or simply take notes in their social studies notebook.
- Students complete a compare/contrast sheet with the ERA on one side and another amendment of their choosing on the other. (Note: Encourage students to choose different amendments so that there are a variety of compare/contrast organizers.)
- Finally, students present these two amendments highlighting what the amendment was for, how long it took to pass, which groups or states were for or against the amendment, and what students' assessment of this process is in light of current-day beliefs.

Lesson: Red Light Green Light
Lesson Outcomes: Students will reflect on the feelings that occur when their options are limited by outside forces.
Grade Levels: Fourth, fifth, and sixth grades
Time Required: Forty to forty-five minutes
Materials: A medium-sized soft ball, small colored strips (two colors, purple and green, equal number of each color), hat or bucket.
Note: This activity may be best conducted outdoors or in the gym.
Methods: Students will play "Red Light Green Light" game with a tweak in the rules.

Equal Rights Amendment

The Equal Rights Amendment (ERA) was first proposed in 1923. Alice Paul first introduced the Equal Rights Amendment to Congress in 1923. The Equal Rights Amendment was written to provide for the legal equality of the sexes and make illegal discrimination on the basis of sex. It took more than 20 years for a vote on the amendment and it was defeated by the full Senate.

In 1967, The National Organization for Women (NOW) took up the fight for the ERA. With the support of feminists Bella Abzug, Betty Friedan and Gloria Steinhem, the ERA won the required two-thirds vote from the U.S. House of Representatives in October 1971. In 1972 it was approved and the Senate sent it to states for approval. For an amendment to be approved, it requires three-fourths of the states. During the mid-1970s the rise of an anti-feminist movement did not pass.

The ERA was reintroduced in 1983 but once again it did not pass. In 2019, the ERA needed only one more state to reach the three-fourths majority to ratify the bill and make it an official amendment to the constitution. There are now 27 amendments to the constitution. Many people hope that the ERA will become the 28th amendment.

Figure 7.2. Equal Rights Amendment

Equal Rights Amendment Timeline

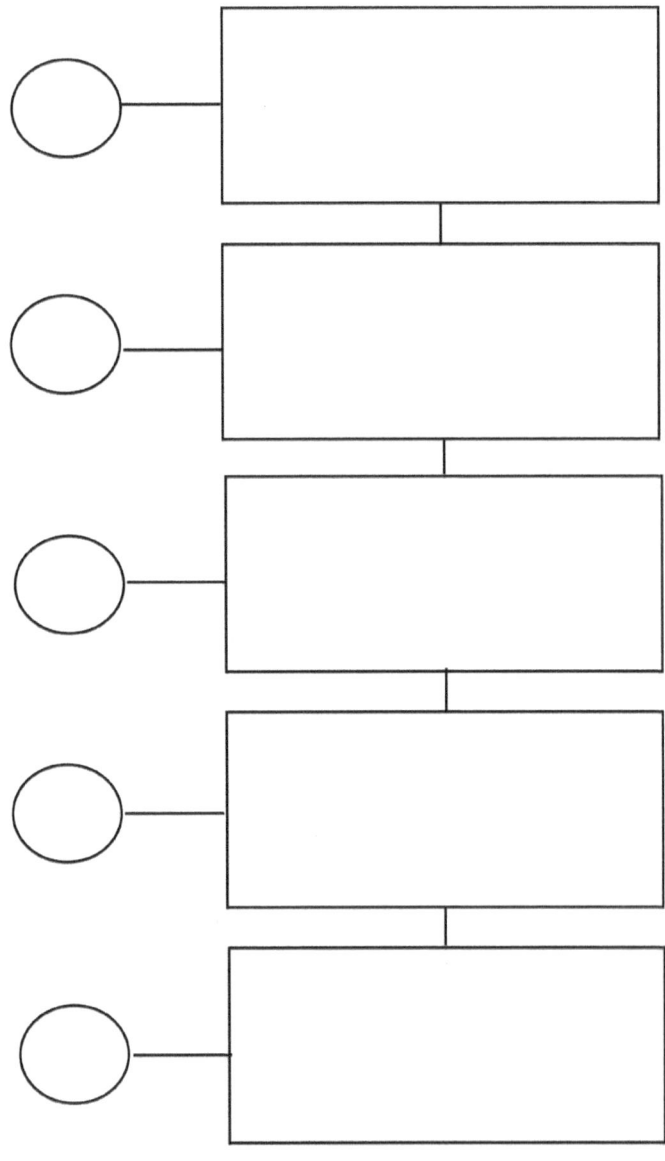

Figure 7.3. Equal Rights Amendment Timeline

- Tell students that they are going to help in a game and an experiment today. The game is "Red Light Green Light," but today we will play it a little bit differently and we will be playing it twice.
- Show students that you are putting green and purple colored strips in the hat and tell them there are an equal number of colors. Pass the hat and ask students to select one strip.
- When all students have selected their strip, tell students to line up for the game.
- Select one student to be "It," or the teacher might choose to fulfill that role.
- Tell the students that the rules for this game will be a little different today. "I'm going to ask you to follow the new rules without any questions. The rule is that those with a purple strip may take only two steps and not run. Those with green strips will run as fast as they can until 'It' says freeze. Then, in the next game, it will be the green strips who have to take only two steps and purple can run as fast as they can." (Note: Students will moan, but tell them "this is an experiment and we are scientists playing this game today.")
- Of course, the students with purple strips in the first game and green strips in the second game won't have a chance of winning because they are being limited by their steps.
- After both games have been completed, ask students how they felt about each game.
- Depending on the age of students, consider the following activities after the game: (1) Write a reflection on how they felt during each game. (2) Talk to a friend and write down three things you felt when you could take only two steps.
- Explain to students that in real life, some people are held back and not given the same privileges as other people. For example, women fought for years for the Equal Rights Amendment to pass, for equal pay for equal work, and to be treated fairly at work. This game gave us a sense of how maybe a lot of women felt in the past and may still feel today.

Lesson: Who and What Is a Feminist?
Lesson Outcomes: Students will understand the definition of feminism and what actions noted feminists have taken to advance the cause of equality for girls and women.
Grade Levels: Third, fourth, fifth, and sixth grades
Time Required: Forty to forty-five minutes
Materials: Biographies of feminists (see resource page), writing paper, or computer

Methods: Students will research the work(s) of a feminist and create a bulletin board and presentation for same-age or younger students.

- Write on the board the definition of feminist: a person who supports political, economic, and social equality of the sexes.
- Tell students that they will be learning about feminists and their work.
- Ask students if they think a boy or a man can be a feminist and lead a discussion on this.
- Encourage students to choose to research a feminist who may not look like them (if possible) so that they can really expand their learning, not just about feminism but maybe about how other people who are different than you might live (example: Malala or Katherine Johnson).
- Instruct students, or provide them with a worksheet, to provide key details about the feminist that can include why they are feminists (what inspired them), what work they did and what the outcomes of their work were.
- Incorporate into their writing any key concepts currently being taught so that this work can be interdisciplinary.
- Upon completion of the writing and editing process, instruct students to either draw a picture of their feminist or to find a photo online to print.
- Consider having students present their work to younger students in the school or to share 1:1 with their younger reading buddies, if they have one.
- Display student work on the bulletin board in a central location and ask the front office to announce that the work is displayed. If possible, have students give a short bio of their feminist during the morning announcement during Women's History Month or at any other time of the year.

Extension Activity: Students create a theatrical production with their feminists as lead characters. Consider engaging the music or art teacher to collaborate on a production. See resource page for more information.

Lesson: Images and Your Brain
Lesson Outcomes: Students will understand how images can affect how people think and what they think about gender.
Grade Levels: Fourth, fifth, and sixth grades
Time Required: Forty to forty-five minutes
Materials: Notebook and a variety of images printed from online sources and magazines. Photos and drawings should be typical photos seen of girls and boys that depict ubiquitous images.
Methods: Students will work in teams to look at a variety of images of girls and boys and determine the messages being sent about that gender.

- Give students in each group/team at least ten photos/drawings of girls. Ask them to just quietly look through them.
- Ask students to now look through the photos to see if there are consistencies across all images. That is, are there themes that they can see across all photos?
- If needed, remind students what consistency and themes mean and provide examples. Example: Show students' photos of puppies and then ask them to name something that the puppies have in common, something that is consistent in all the photos. Some answers might include young, cute, friendly, cuddly, and fun.
- After students have had time to take notes about consistencies/themes of photos and drawings of girls, give them at least ten photos of boys.
- Ask students to do the same activity with the photos of boys.
- When students have completed taking notes for both boys and girls, ask for volunteers to report on their findings. What words did they write down about the photos of girls and then boys?
- Ask students if they see similar images during the day and to give an estimate of about how many times per week.
- To integrate math into the lesson, have students then calculate how many times in a year they are seeing similar images.
- Teach students about how implicit biases are formed, even against one's own race or gender.
- Ask students in what ways they can counter the impact of these types of images. Some suggestions may include writing to advertisers and manufacturers to ask them to provide more varied images in their material, finding other products to use or images to look at (actively seeking out diverse experiences), and creating visual displays for the school in which girls and boys are seen in a much wider lens with more varied images.

Chapter Eight

Intersectionality

When considering how to lift the burden of gender limitations for students, educators would benefit from also acknowledging the layers of limitations that students face in addition to gender. Students may face not only the limitations brought on by poverty and internal struggles of figuring out identity, but also because of the implicit biases against each and every one of the layers that make up who they are.

GENDER IDENTITY AND LANGUAGE

Elementary teachers use and feel the power of language in their daily teaching. Throughout the day, teachers and students examine words and their meanings and consider how expressive read-aloud books can make a story come to life. Whether it's deciphering the words in a math problem or using context clues in a reading passage, students are surrounded by words and their meanings all day. This practice includes words that others may internalize to define who they are. Sometimes, those words can help students feel encouraged and expansive, and other times, words can carry the burdensome weight of bias.

It is not a label or word itself that results in biased treatment, but instead the unspoken meanings behind them. When a person thinks or says the word *girl* and that brings to mind words like *pretty*, *feminine*, and *compliant*, then that girl has been assigned attributes she might neither appreciate nor accept. If words like *strong*, *controlled*, and *active* define the word *boy*, then the expectation is that the boy will have those characteristics which may not be even close to defining him.

Language and labels impact how we think about gender and what we think about individual people defined as one gender or another. Adding other layers of race, ethnicity, socioeconomic status, and sexual orientation to words also adds layers of bias. Several studies have been done to determine the impact of gender-based grammar and thought. In these studies, researchers asked participants to assign descriptions of words in their own language.

With many languages assigning a feminine or masculine to nouns, it is not surprising that *car* in Spanish (masculine *el coche*) would be described with typical male characteristics. The word chair in French (feminine *la chaise*) would be described with typical feminine characteristics. It makes sense that if a noun is assigned a gender and people have automatic associations with gender, then there is an automatic or unconscious association between the two.

One gender linguistic study, however, went further by asking Spanish- and German-speaking participants to describe objects in English. These participants were fluent in English, but unlike their native language, nouns in English have no gender assignment. The objects they were asked to describe held the opposite gender in each language. For instance, in one language *chair* might be feminine and in the other masculine. Spanish and German speakers assigned adjectives that were more masculine for items whose names were grammatically masculine in their native language than for items whose names were grammatically feminine.

All object words in the study had opposite genders in Spanish and German; Spanish and German speakers produced very different adjectives to describe the objects. For items that were grammatically masculine in Spanish but feminine in German, adjectives provided by Spanish speakers were rated more masculine than those provided by German speakers.[1] Assigning gender to a noun had a clear and direct connection to thinking about that noun and its gender-related description, even when a second genderless language was used.

These studies have educational implications for what they teach about how a simple word can influence thinking. While in the English language, most nouns are not assigned a gender, the nouns *boy* and *girl* conjure up specific images and attributes. A boy is far more likely to bring to mind words like *powerful*, *smart*, and *strong*. It seems almost inconceivable to think of words like *compliant* and *lovely* when hearing the word *boy*. It does not require grammatical differentiation for boys and girls to quickly understand what the expectations of them are because of their word that describes their gender role.

Most children in elementary school would answer that they were a boy or a girl if asked. But the list of ways that some students feel different can be long and sometimes confusing. They may understand the cultural definition of their birth sex, but not exactly feel like they think they should. From an early age, because of the definitions assigned to boy and girl, children can feel either completely aligned with the definition, completed alienated from it, or somewhere in between.

Rather than get rid of labels that often don't accurately define or fully encompass who people are, more definitions are arriving into our language to even further delineate this from that, you from me. While all these new terms can be confusing, perhaps in looking at all the ways people are different, people can circle back around to recognize that despite the differences, the commonality is in people's humanity. Still, there is a new gender-based vocabulary to be mindful of, even for elementary teachers, and a comprehensive list can be found in the resources chapter.

NONBINARY VOCABULARY

One fairly new gender term is *nonbinary*. This term means that a person neither feels male nor female. And it is within this term that perhaps some answers to navigating the more complex issues of gender can be found. The National Center for Transgender Equality has recommendations for understanding and supporting nongender people. Their recommendations include:

- Use the name a person asks you to use.
- Don't make assumptions about people's gender.
- If you're not sure what pronouns someone uses, ask.
- Talk to nonbinary people to find out more about who they are.

Asking these types of questions without any prejudgment may feel very much like an approach to use with all people on many topics, not just gender. A person may decide to change their name because it never seemed to fit their personality or their look, not just their gender. Approaching someone without assumptions is always a good idea, and getting to know someone, whether that's about their gender identity or any other personal topic is fundamental in relationship building. These recommendations are also fitting reminders of maintaining a caring and loving position with students as the world is rapidly changing.

The use of different pronouns can definitely be challenging. Remembering each student's name and preferred nickname, specific learning needs, food allergies, friendship issues, and personalities are just a handful of things to catalog in the teacher's mind. If individual students adopt different pronouns, how can any teacher keep up with all of this? Considering the heavy weight of implicit biases might help. What might bring this into greater focus is questioning if these new factors to consider are feeling burdensome because it's one more thing to address or because we are internally uncomfortable with those changes.

Even if a teacher has no reason to consider using a pronoun that is gender free, the topic is worthy of some further consideration for what the use of pronouns can teach us. What if instead of using pronouns, we referred to students more frequently by their name or the collective "we" to distribute focus or to build community? Consider seemingly innocuous daily encounters and how the use of language and gender-based words or gender-free words might change the emotional punch of an interaction.

John: Ms. Smith, why is Haley crying? She cries a lot.

Ms. Smith: Haley is upset. Sometimes, we have to cry to feel our emotions.

If Ms. Smith had said "she has to cry" instead of "we have to cry," John may have interpreted this as being an action carried out by just Haley or just girls. By using *we* instead of *she*, the message is that crying can be done by anyone. Ms. Smith goes further to not only explain that crying is an action that anyone can do, but that it also helps all of us feel our emotions.

Expressing emotion can be then elevated from something weak people do (aka girls) or an action that should cause embarrassment, to an action that serves a purpose. In that one interaction Ms. Smith has diverted attention away from the student crying, attempted to form a community through the use of *we* and taught about the value of the action being witnessed. Sometimes, a small change like a pronoun can be profound.

GENDER-FLUIDITY EDUCATION – TRENDS AND GUIDELINES

Before assigning new pronouns or addressing students by a more preferred gender name, most educators would meet with parents to learn more, assess a child's perceptions about gender identity, and discuss how to proceed. Elementary educators, in particular, want to ensure that there is common ground on any approach. In addition to parent meetings, however, educators need to be mindful of not only parents but also the government regulations that are currently in place, ones that just passed legislation, and revisions that may take place as a result of reflection of community objections.

In the spring of 2019, the state of California approved a new framework for sex education in the classroom that stirred great debate about the graphic and explicit nature of the material. Some parents of elementary students maintain that the public school system has gone too far in teaching their children about gender fluidity and transgender children. They have become politically active, calling for legislative interventions to curtail changes.

Hundreds of California parents protested the new framework that included books entitled, *My Princess Boy* and *Who Are You? The Kids Guide to Gender Identity*. Both these books were assigned to students as young as first grade within the curriculum guidelines. After public protests, these two books and several others were removed.[2] When considering an action plan for a gender-equity initiative, take into account those who may be in agreement on the concept, but disagree on the implementation.

Senator Brian Jones of California joined the parent protest. "The parent-child relationship is sacred and special to each family, and parents and guardians know what is best for their children. Yet, the State Board of Education is attacking our liberty with its disgusting and unintellectual proposal to teach controversial sex practices and education to children as young as 6 years old!"[3]

In June 2019, New York City made policy changes within "Guidelines for Supporting Transgender and Gender Expansive Students." Students will be able to change their name and gender on school records with a parent's or guardian's permission, without legal documentation. Families will also be able to self-report their child's gender upon enrolling in a New York City Department of Education School.[4]

While New York and California are liberal coastal states that don't always represent national trends, the federal Department of Education has issued guidelines for all public schools with regard to gender identity rights and they are based on the Title IX law. "No person in the United States shall, on the basis of sex, be excluded from participation in, be denied the benefits of, or be subjected to discrimination under any education program or activity receiving Federal financial assistance."[5]

Educators look to both federal and local governments for guidelines on issues of civil rights, social justice, and the rights of students in schools. The guidelines, laws, and frameworks on gender equity are evolving. As seen in California, government initiatives can be perceived as treading on privacy and parental rights and responsibilities and subsequently revised on strong public opinion. Other states follow federal guidelines and take a wait-and-see approach to the trends and laws being passed.

It is no doubt a challenging topic for educators trying to navigate relatively new topics of civil rights and to balance those rights with parental input, laws, particular school policy, and personal concerns for students and their identities. There is lots of noise on the topic. Students who can count on educators to take in the discussion without being overwhelmed by the noise will benefit from the support of a well-educated and caring school community. As with many other personal topics, educators who are willing to respect the questions that students are raising about gender will strengthen opportunities for other areas of learning.

Chapter 8

INTERSECTIONALITY—GIRLS AND RACISM

> The way we imagine discrimination or disempowerment often is more complicated for people who are subjected to multiple forms of exclusion. The good news is that intersectionality provides us a way to see it.
> —Kimberlé Crenshaw

In exploring the ways that children feel limited by their gender, it is essential to look at the additional layers of bias that many students encounter. Intersectional Feminism refers to the layers of discrimination that some people face in addition to gender. Consider the black girl in a largely white community who not only faces biases because of her gender, but also her race. Adding poverty and sexual identity, that child can be faced with multiple layers of bias and struggle because of her identity, assigned labels, and the perception of who she is because of those labels.

Kimberlé Crenshaw is credited with the term *intersectionality* through her teaching and public speaking. Despite being assigned credit for coining the term, Crenshaw acknowledges the many black women activists that came before her for the inspiration and for being instruments of change.[6] The struggle to be seen and for the biases to be seen has been a long one.

According a 2015 study, school experiences for black girls differ from black boys and most certainly from white girls.[7] Many studies, including "Black Girls Matter: Pushed Out, Overpoliced and Underprotected," focus largely on the high school years, but the different treatment of black girls begins as early as preschool. These signs of different treatment are important indicators for elementary teachers to address so that opportunities to address inequities can begin early in the school years.

In this study, Kimberlé Crenshaw reports, "This silence about at-risk girls is multidimensional and cross-institutional. The risks that black and other girls of color confront rarely receive the full attention of researchers, advocates, policy makers, and funders. As a result, many educators, activists, and community members remain underinformed about the consequences of punitive school policies on girls as well as the distinctly gendered dynamics of zero-tolerance environments that limit their educational achievements."

The report goes on to show that black girls face a statistically greater chance of suspension and expulsion compared to other students of the same gender. While this prevalence of racial disparity is well known, it has not been highlighted as a significant factor of *both* racial and gender discrimination. Factors that may contribute to the scant reporting about this issue include methods of data gathering and the failure to report information by both race and gender.

Reports that do disaggregate data to reveal the status of boys often fail to report the available data on girls, leaving the impression that black girls are not facing significant race/gender issues. There are, however, some statistics available and they paint a bleak picture. A 2015 report by the US Department of Education for Civil Rights provides includes the following data:[8]

- While they are just 16 percent of America's female student population, black girls account for more than 33 percent of all female arrests that take place on our school campuses, according to data from the Education Department's office for civil rights.
- While black boys receive more than two out of three suspensions, black girls are suspended at higher rates (12 percent) than girls of any other race or ethnicity and most boys.
- Black children represent 18 percent of preschool enrollment, but 48 percent of preschool children receiving more than one out-of-school suspension; in comparison, white students represent 43 percent of preschool enrollment but 26 percent of preschool children receiving school suspension.

The statistic on the suspension of preschool children illustrates that the school-to-prison pipeline can begin early. And the pipeline can include more than prison. Black girls face confinement in detention centers, house arrests, electronic monitoring, and other forms of punishment and exclusion from society.[9]

The information provided through reports like Crenshaw's and the Department of Education shine a light on the stark differences in discipline of black girls. For educators who are using the Listening and Looking Assessments and are teaching black girls, some modifications that include intersectionality can provide additional needed school-specific data to address implicit bias in the classroom. Questions that can be included:

- If girls are called to answer less frequently than boys, how much less are black girls called on to answer?
- Are black girls disciplined/corrected more frequently in the class for the same offenses as white girls?
- Is it possible that cultural differences are leading to misunderstandings, poor communication, or biased perceptions?
- What new learning can I do to ensure that my black female students feel heard and respected?

As educators review the gender-equity lessons for students in this book, they may also consider how ideas of gender equity and intersectionality can be woven into them. When creating a visual culture, students can be encouraged to find accomplished black women (see resources chapter for more information) or think about how lessons can change to effectively speak to students who may feel marginalized.

INTERSECTIONALITY—RACISM

Intersectionality addresses the layers of bias and discrimination suffered by girls and women beyond gender alone. Studies show how an added layer of racism affects students' self-concepts and confidence. A child who is born a girl and girl of color presents that child with two forms of bias that she will face throughout her day, including school. This bias can have serious implications for academic success.

Psychologists Claude Steele and Joshua Aronson found that black students who were told that an exam was diagnostic of intellectual capacity performed worse on the exam compared with whites. The difference did not appear for black students who were told that the exam was not diagnostic of intellect.[10] The negative effects of stereotype threat have also been demonstrated in Latino students [11]

"Race-based disparities in stress and sleep in context model (RDSSC), which argues that racial/ethnic disparities in educational achievement and attainment are partially explained by the effects of race-based stressors, such as stereotype threat and perceived discrimination, on psychological and biological responses to stress, which, in turn, impact cognitive functioning and academic performance."[12]

INTERSECTIONALITY: SOCIOECONOMIC STATUS

Another layer that can be added to gender bias is the layer of poverty. A student from a low income household has multiple challenges in finding success in school. Poor students are less likely to visit doctors and receive adequate medical help. Food available to these students tend to be of a lower nutritional value and this can affect development in the womb.[13] Students with poor nutrition and health have a harder time listening and learning. Poor nutrition, such as a diet in highly processed or sugar-laden foods, can also affect behavior which can lead to ineffective discipline practices because the student has little control over the causes of this behavior.

Just as the statistics show that black girls are suspended at a greater rate than white girls or boys, there's a similar outcome for poor children. They get, on average, twice as many reprimands as compliments. This is in contrast to middle-class students who receive three positive comments for every negative one.[14] Considering the findings about poor nutrition, health, and related attention, energy and focus issues for these students are an inevitable outcome. Educators and students both benefit when additional factors are investigated about the behavior and motivation of students who face layers of intersectionality.

INTERSECTIONALITY: GIRLS WITH DISABILITIES

The Individuals with Disabilities Education Act (IDEA) of 1975 mandates that children with disabilities be educated in the "least restricted environment," meaning a setting that affords the students the maximum opportunities to learn, socialize, and interact with students without disabilities, while still meeting each child's individual needs. Reports on the special education systems reveal challenges to meeting the mandate.

> With an increasing number of children requiring special education services in the schools, significant demands are being placed on both special and regular education teachers. Learners with differing educational, behavioral, and medical needs are both financially and emotionally challenging for both their school districts and teachers alike. School budgets are being depleted rapidly as districts attempt to provide a free and appropriate education (FAPE) for all, especially when Individualized Education Plans (IEP) require extensive special services including speech, physical, occupational therapy, nursing, counseling, behavioral services, in-class support, and personal aides.[15]

There is very little research on gender and special education but a great deal of research on special education and race. What is known, however, is that far fewer girls than boys receive special education services, making up about one-third of students served.[16] Three theories have been put forward to explain the gender differences in special education identification rates: (1) biological differences between girls and boys, (2) behavioral differences between girls and boys, and (3) bias in special education referral and assessment procedures.[17]

Boys are more likely than girls to exhibit problematic behavioral characteristics. These behaviors may indicate the existence of a disability or need for testing. By acting out, boys may be more likely to gain the attention of adults, making them more easily identifiable as learning challenged. Boys are most often referred to special education for behavioral problems, not for their underlying disabilities.[18]

Girls who are identified as possessing emotional disabilities are typically processed through special education only after they exhibit behaviors that are typical of male students who already receive special education. This "one size fits all" approach to identification ignores the possibility that assessment instruments may be poorly designed and do not detect some emotional problems (i.e., depression) that are more prevalent in girls than boys.[19]

Chapter 8

MYTH OF AVERAGE REVISITED

The myth of average was explored in chapter 1 within the scope of one form of bias: gender. As additional levels of bias are examined, the myth of average becomes even more salient. When looking for the average, educators are trying to establish a baseline from which to grow. This search is not only understandable on a human level, but mandated on state and federal levels.

Educators are in the business of teaching academics, and to do so, there need to be goals and those goals are based on research about what the "average" child can do. Further, those goals, so often set by the federal or state governments, set into motion a way to judge teachers as well. The idea being that an average fourth-grade student can learn and reach certain benchmarks, so the average fourth-grade teacher needs to ensure that the child can in fact grow in this way. Students and teachers can both feel trapped in this search for the average.

The benchmarks are based on the average, but if children have no average, how can all of those benchmarks be met? Can students who feel marginalized and under the stress of implicit bias, whether that's from gender alone or layers of bias on top of that threat, perform as well as a student for whom the system was built? In many cases, the answer to that question is that they simply cannot.

The layers of bias students feel can impact their behavior and academic performance. Implicit bias resides in every person, including teachers. A teacher who believes that the average girl should behave a certain way can have bias about a girl who exhibits behaviors that appear to the teacher more appropriate for a boy. A teacher who believes that the results of living in poverty are really about laziness may have a fixed mindset based on many things she heard as a child, rather than something that is true. And adding to those feelings is the pressure of being judged on the performance of children struggling to grow at the rate set as the average.

In a school system that is built for the average, biases can become part of that system and the students may be seen as problems. Boys are receiving intervention services more for behavior issues than academic ones, and girls are receiving less. Black girls are disciplined more, often starting from as early as preschool with implicit biases very real but poorly understood. Does the average school simply not fit the boy with boundless energy and are girls who struggle to receive not getting services because they are quiet and compliant? Are black girls disciplined more because of cultural mismatches with teachers or are behavior issues born from stereotype threat?

A teacher leading a diverse classroom of students has monumental tasks to complete effectively each day. Managing the lives of tens of students, keeping them safe and ensuring that all students receive the specific instruction they need requires careful thought and professionalism. Taking the time to learn about the impact of racism, intersectionality, statistics on special education services, and the weight of gender expectations is a means to a more productive and fruitful end. As part of the reflective process on student growth, asking the following questions has the potential to reach students who before seemed unreachable.

- What is it about that black girl's behavior that I find threatening or unacceptable and how much of that is based on my own bias? In what ways can I connect with her? In what ways might my classroom be making her feel like it's a bad fit?
- Is that boy in my class really ready for a referral or are there ways I can redesign my classroom to create more movement in the class and opportunities for more student talk? How can I work with his parents to encourage more movement, more reading, and less videos after school?
- Is that student who never talks simply shy or is she quietly struggling to understand what is going on in this classroom? Has she internalized messages about her gender that leave her feeling unable to speak?
- What can I learn about gender stereotypes, biases, and intersectionality that can enrich my practice and help support my students in reaching their full potential?

Regularly posing questions like these is not a means toward guaranteeing a perfect outcome for all students. It is a means of modifying a teaching practice so it can result in more productive outcomes for students and student growth. Children are reminded hundreds of times throughout their early years that they are different from one another. They internalize the message: "You are this. I am that." In addition to the more cultural definition of what it means to be a girl or a boy, race, socioeconomic status, gender identity, and ethnicity further define what it means to be *that* boy or girl.

For students in our current culture, that means there will be limitations about how they are perceived or what they think they can do. Their self-esteem and self-efficacy can be supported by educators who see the layers of bias, who modify to lift the weight of bias, and who do not look for the average student, but look at the students in front of them. Supporting equitable treatment of students helps them reach their goal of self-efficacy and can move students from feeling marginalized to boundless.

NOTES

1. Toshi Konishi, "The Semantics of Grammatical Gender: A Cross-Cultural Study," *Journal of Psycholinguistic Research* 22, no. 5 (1993): 519–34, https://doi.org/10.1007/bf01068252.
2. "Health Education Framework," Health Education (California Department of Education), accessed December 16, 2019, https://www.cde.ca.gov/ci/he/cf/.

3. "Informed Parents of California Rally," Senator Brian Jones, April 2, 2019, https://jones.cssrc.us/content/informed-parents-california-rally-0.

4. "Chancellor Carranza Announces Updated Transgender and First-Ever Gender Inclusion Guidelines for New York City Schools," accessed December 16, 2019, https://www.schools.nyc.gov/about-us/news/announcements/contentdetails/2019/06/28/chancellor-carranza-announces-updated-transgender-and-first-ever-gender-inclusion-guidelines-for-new-york-city-schools.

5. "Title IX and Sex Discrimination," US Department of Education, September 25, 2018, https://www2.ed.gov/about/offices/list/ocr/docs/tix_dis.html.

6. "What Does Intersectional Feminism Actually Mean?," IWDA, November 8, 2018, https://iwda.org.au/what-does-intersectional-feminism-actually-mean/?gclid=CjwKCAiAlO7uBRANEiwA_vXQ-2DGueLO1lRFRBgEy6ZJNPb-3Lr7EXWSMEL_4CdK0emZ34d0kiO-ARoC-D8QAvD_BwE.

7. "Publications," AAPF, accessed December 16, 2019, http://aapf.org/publications.

8. US Department of Education Report: "Civil Rights Data Collection," accessed December 16, 2019, https://ocrdata.ed.gov/.

9. "Understanding Non-Binary People: How to Be Respectful and Supportive," National Center for Transgender Equality, October 5, 2018, https://transequality.org/issues/resources/understanding-non-binary-people-how-to-be-respectful-and-supportive.

10. American Psychological Association, "Stereotype Threat Widens Achievement Gap," accessed December 16, 2019, https://www.apa.org/research/action/stereotype.

11. Patricia M. Gonzales, Hart Blanton, and Kevin J. Williams, "The Effects of Stereotype Threat and Double-Minority Status on the Test Performance of Latino Women," *Personality and Social Psychology Bulletin* 28, no. 5 (2002): 659–70, https://doi.org/10.1177/0146167202288010.

12. Dorainne J. Levy, Jennifer A. Heissel, Jennifer A. Richeson, and Emma K. Adam, "Psychological and Biological Responses to Race-Based Social Stress as Pathways to Disparities in Educational Outcomes," *American Psychologist* 71, no. 6 (2016): 455–73, https://doi.org/10.1037/a0040322.

13. J. Neu, "Vulnerability of the Fetal Primate Brain to Moderate Reduction in Maternal Global Nutrient Availability," *Yearbook of Neonatal and Perinatal Medicine* (2011): 56–58, https://doi.org/10.1016/j.ynpm.2011.07.106.

14. American Psychological Association, accessed December 16, 2019, https://psycnet.apa.org/record/1995-98.

15. Sheri Marino Ma and Linda Fassberg, "The Special Ed Epidemic: Burying Our Heads and Crippling Our Economy," Focus for Health, September 10, 2019, https://www.focusforhealth.org/part-2-the-special-ed-epidemic-burying-our-heads-and-crippling-our-economy/.

16. US Department of Education, Office of Special Education Programs, and Westat, July 15, 2007, Table 1-12: Children and Students Served under IDEA, Part B, in the U.S. and Outlying Areas, by Gender and Age Group, accessed January 14, 2009, http://www.ideadata.org/tables30th/ar_1-12.htm.

17. M. J. Coutinho, D. P. Oswald, and M. King, "Differences in the Special Education Identification Rates for Boys and Girls: Trends and Issues," (2001): 27–30.

18. M. L. Wehmeyer and M. Schwartz, "Research on Gender Bias in Special Education Services," in *Double Jeopardy: Addressing Gender Equity in Special Education*, ed. H. Rousso and M. Wehmeyer (Albany, NY: State University of New York Press, 2001).

19. Congressional Research Service, "Individuals with Disabilities Education Act: Identification and Misidentification of Children with Disabilities" (No. RL31189) (Washington, DC: Apling, 2001).

Chapter Nine

Looking to Their Future

It is common for staff rooms to be filled with teachers speculating about their students' lives as adults. Where will they live and what jobs will they have are just a few of the aspects of students' lives that are considered and talked about. Because education is ripe with benchmarks and goals to reach, it is natural that looking forward, the eye is on one prize—achievement. The one important concept that is not as often predicted is that of personal fulfillment and happiness.

That is far more difficult to define, to measure, and to predict. Perhaps there are few adults who take time to think about ideas of fulfillment and happiness in their own lives. Goals are often developed on the basis of what people do rather than who they are or the level of meaning in their lives. While achievements are often intertwined with happiness for many individuals, sometimes the person can get lost in favor of the material or professional accomplishments.

If it were possible to time travel back twenty years, elementary teachers might be observed having similar conversations as teachers do today when discussing their students' future. If those teachers twenty years ago had the chance to look at today's research and data on gender, would their approach to students be different? Would their lessons be modified based on reflecting on the uphill climb many students face?

Instead of just pride in that fourth-grade student who became a doctor, would there also be wonder about how that doctor's self-concepts were holding up? Was that doctor also comfortable in her own skin, free from stereotype threat? Was there something about gender expectations that drove that girl's ability to find her own path rather than just follow the one someone else carved out for her?

Teachers cannot ensure students' futures or level of happiness. However, what takes place in school is part of children's cultural upbringing and development of self-efficacy. Their interactions with each other, with the adults in schools, and the images they are exposed to are the building blocks for how they see themselves. This time of life in elementary school can have a significant impact on the shaping of children's futures.

GIRLS/WOMEN

According to a 2019 report issued by the United States Census Bureau, the gender pay gap widens among men and women when women have a bachelor's degree. For those without a degree, women make seventy-eight cents for every dollar a man makes. For those with a degree, pay drops to seventy-four cents for every dollar a man makes. "Higher pay reflects years of work experience and pay raises. The earnings differences between men and women also peak in their 50s, although men on average earn more at every age than their female counterparts." Pay is not the only way women are discriminated against. There is also inequity in opportunities.[1]

As of 2019,

- Six percent of the Fortune 500 chief executive officers are women.
- Twenty-five percent of the Senate is comprised of women.
- Eighteen percent of all states' governors are women.
- In movies, only 33 percent of all speaking roles were filled by girls or women. Females were far more likely than their male counterparts in 2018 to be shown in sexually revealing attire (29.2 vs. 7.4 percent) and with some nudity (27.3 vs. 8.5 percent). Girls/women were also more likely than boys/men to be referenced as attractive by other characters (10.2 vs. 2.7 percent).[2]

Women, on average, earn less than men in every single occupation. In middle-skill occupations (jobs that don't require a bachelor's degree), women will get paid 66 percent of what a man makes in a comparable field when the jobs are filled with a majority of women. If change continues to happen at the same rate as it has been, pay equality will be not reached until 2059 for non-Hispanic or non-Black women. For Hispanic women, the pay gap won't be closed until 2224 and for Black women not until 2130.[3]

These statistics are just a few that represent the level of inequity in the United States across companies and public office. As our brains seek to categorize and associate information, the images it is processing is of many men and boys in positions of power and women and girls often in supporting roles. Unless a greater balance is achieved within the workplace and schools, we will continue to make those same associations.

As described in chapter 1, our reactions often belie our automatic thoughts and reactions. One part of the brain is working for efficiency (I see lots of men in power; therefore, men *should be* in positions of power). Unless girls and boys begin seeing these images of diverse female and male achievement, the implicit biases that send the message that girls have less value than boys will be reinforced. How that can change is by clearly seeing what is happening, how implicit bias is formed out of prior experiences and information, and then consciously choosing to take action to create a more equitable experience for all genders.

What do these free associations the brain make have to do with happiness? As can be seen in the statistics on women in the workforce, there is insufficient association with accomplishment and instead an association with unfairness. If a young woman's dream is to direct a film, there are far more roadblocks ahead of her than if she were a young man. Replace that industry with hundreds of others and the results would be quite similar. Reduced opportunities make one's life smaller and more stressful.

American women are twice as likely to suffer from an anxiety disorder as men. While studies have not demonstrated a direct correlation between the following statistics and anxiety, they are certainly worthy of note. Women who are full-time workers earn about 25 percent less than male counterparts in a given year. The poverty rate for women aged eighteen to sixty-four is 14.2 percent compared with 10.5 percent for men. About one in three women have experienced sexual violence, physical violence, and/or stalking by an intimate partner in their lifetime. An estimated 65 percent of caregivers are women. Female caregivers may spend as much as 50 percent more time providing care than male caregivers.[4]

It's not possible to precisely predict how changes in elementary instruction might impact girls' feelings about themselves as adults. However, educators do know the value of role models. Creating lessons that include accomplished and well-adjusted women, modeling gender fairness, and adopting measured and gender-healthy teaching practices are effective ways to send important and powerful messages about potential.

Recent research has shown that despite advances for women, happiness for women has declined over the past few decades. Some accounting for this is that while women are achieving more, they are also doing more. While stepping out of the traditional roles requires thoughtful and conscious decision making, men and women may very well still be unconsciously associating women with caretaking and domestic roles. So while women have greater opportunities, they are also taking on greater amounts of work and stress.

For teachers and students, learning about the brain and its functions can be liberating. Understanding implicit bias is like going behind the scenes of a movie watching as the amygdala perpetuates the status quo scanning for repeated patterns. While that is happening, the prefrontal and frontal cortex portions of the brain allow for decision making. Simply knowing that can generate a new approach to old ways of reacting and unwarranted assumptions. Rather than just blindly acting upon multiple old scenes, perhaps knowing the brain mechanics of implicit bias may prompt thought rather than automaticity or reaction. Resources to learn more about the brain are located in chapter 10.

BOYS/MEN

Watching boys gather on a ball field, reading books in the library, or stretched out on the living room sofa, it would be hard to believe that the messages they are receiving are putting them in harm's way and creating stress levels that are hard to bear. It's hard to believe because it is a common occurrence for boys to hide their feelings. It is what they are trained to do from the legacy passed down through the generations. It is part of their cultural thumbprint.

The potential for toxicity in manhood has been explored through organizations like A Call to Men and books such as *The Boy Crisis* by Farrell and Gray and *Real Boys* by Pollack. Increasing attention is being paid to the mask boys wear as leaders who are strong and protective. For many boys, this armor is a heavy and burdensome weight to carry.

"Confused by society's mixed messages about what's expected of them as boys, and later as men, many feel a sadness and disconnection they cannot even name. New research shows that boys are doing less well than they did in the past and in comparison to girls, that many boys have remarkably fragile self-esteem, and that the rates of depression and suicide in boys are frighteningly on the rise."[5]

In 2017, men died by suicide nearly four times more often than women. White males account for nearly 70 percent of all male deaths and suicide among middle-age white men in particular.[6] Suicide is the second leading cause of death in the world for those aged fifteen to twenty-four years.[7] These statistics do not paint the picture of powerful and in control men. Rather this data calls for some clarity on the stereotype threat that men face and the dire consequences that may be connected to it.

In chapter 2, a hierarchy of needs depicts what it might look like when including gender-healthy development. In *The Boy Crisis*, Farrell's Hierarchy of the Traditional Male Hero's Values is illustrated in Figure 9.1. This pyramid does not include self-actualization as a top need. In fact, it is nowhere to be found. Self-actualization can become an impossible challenge for men who have been trained primarily for accomplishment and success.

"What Maslow describes as the most basic needs—food, water, safety—are needs the male hero only allows himself as a means to an end: to have the strength to kill the dragon. Whether he is a marine, Navy SEAL, or firefighter, the hero only allows himself to indulge in safety, warmth, and the rest for his own personal comfort *after* his missions are accomplished. In the traditional male hero's hierarchy of needs, self-actualization is nowhere to be found because the more he values himself, the less he is willing to sacrifice himself."[8]

CONSTRUCTING A NEW UNDERSTANDING

The way gender is presented is so ubiquitous that people don't often employ metacognition about gender at all. If very common images, literary content and conversations about men include super heroes, and related leadership, protectiveness, and strength and women's are nurturing, emotional and fragile, and often sexual, then those messages are creating a thumbprint on the brain. These thumbprints on people's brains are created from a very early age

Safety, warmth
and rest
Being a dominant, revered,
kind and wise force
Being a dominant, feared force
Survival (but not safety), food, water
Belongingness and Love Needs: Winning the hand of a beautiful woman in marriage by protecting and providing for her and the children.
Respect and Approval Needs: Trying to get society's respect by fulfilling what society expects of him, even if that means being killed in war or dying from stress from overwork

Figure 9.1. Farrell's Hierarchy of the Traditional Male Hero's Values *Source:* From Dr. Warren Farrell's *The Boy Crisis* (Dallas: BenBella, 2018), reprinted with permission from Dr. Farrell.

and continue to be reinforced and built upon in multiple interactions throughout each and every day.

While social construct makes it seem that people have the ability to change it if they want to, the thoughts about gender become so ingrained and automatic, their conscious beliefs might actually disagree quite strongly with the thumbprint. But it is not the conscious belief that dictates most of our actions, but the unconscious thumbprint. The social construct today isn't benign in our culture. The social construct based on thumbprints on the brain limits children's ability to self-actualize because there are limits and expectations that don't always fit with who individuals are or who they want to be.

When limited numbers of leaders, parents, and teachers are aware of how these implicit biases form, then change will be limited and situational. With great numbers of people looking at their own implicit biases and making thoughtful decisions to counter those biases, then real and lasting change can happen. Educators who are committed to new learning and integrating gender equity initiatives into "whole child" education can make seismic impacts on children's futures.

Using the Listening and Looking Assessments in chapter 2 is a great place to start. Getting to know one's own biases, looking at teaching practices, and considering positive changes can increase the gender health of classrooms, teams, and schools. Creating a written document to plot a course of action will enable teachers and administrators to firm up the commitment for the current school year and beyond. Fostering a collaborative environment so that all adults, administrators, teachers, and parents can feel safe in speaking about their implicit biases is a powerful step that can long lasting impact.

Educators are powerful role models and resources to influence positive change. Not only can they create nurturing classrooms and schools, they have the power to spread the word to parents and communities. Many schools have proven their commitment to children through advocacy for character education programs, inclusive teaching practices, and food for hungry children in their care. It's time to include a gender-healthy environment into that commitment. Extending that commitment to gender equity takes an open heart to new learning, an end to thinking about who the average girl or boy is, and a devotion to breaking down walls that limit who children can become.

NOTES

1. https://www.census.gov/library/stories/2019/05/college-degree-widens-gender-earnings-gap.html.

2. https://womenandhollywood.com/resources/statistics/2018-statistics/.

3. Valerie Lacarte, Cynthia Hess, and Ariane Hegewisch, "Pay Equity & Discrimination," Institute for Women's Policy Research, September 11, 2019, https://iwpr.org/issue/employment-education-economic-change/pay-equity-discrimination/.

4. file:///C:/Users/doven/Downloads/Mental-Health-Facts-for-Women.pdf.
5. William Pollack, *Real Boys: Rescuing Our Sons from the Myths of Boyhood* (New York: Henry Holt, 1999).
6. "Suicide Statistics." AFSP, April 16, 2019, https://afsp.org/about-suicide/suicide-statistics/.
7. "Suicide Statistics and Facts," SAVE, accessed December 16, 2019, https://save.org/about-suicide/suicide-facts/.
8. Warren Farrell and John Gray, *The Boy Crisis: Why Our Boys Are Struggling and What We Can Do about It* (Dallas, TX: BenBella Books, 2019).

Chapter Ten

Resources

On the following pages are resources and links for educators that provide background and statistics on gender-related issues. The categories are organized for teachers and their students who may be of a specific gender or living with different levels of overt or implicit bias. There are also resources for educators teaching women's history and resources mentioned in the professional development lessons from chapter 4.

The resources on the gendered brain are the most current as of this book's publication date. With brain research in its relative infancy and new research being conducted on an ongoing basis, those who are interested in keeping up to date should seek out the latest published works by leaders in the field. Following the works of Gina Rippon, Diane Halpern, and Larry Cahill will keep educators apprised of the latest research on gender and the brain.

Finally, there is the glossary of terms that define the words and phrases used around gender and related concepts currently in use today. There are many terms to be aware of and terms that may have different definitions or interpretations depending on who is using them. These words and terms would generally not be used in interactions between most elementary grade level students and teachers. However, as children grow toward the intermediary grades, they may begin to question labels and terms or use them in ways that require clarification.

GENERAL RESOURCES FOR EDUCATORS

NOW—National Organization for Women describes itself as a grassroots movement dedicated to the multiple issues surrounding women's rights. It is the largest feminist grassroots organization in the United States. NOW has hundreds of chapters and thousands of members in all fifty states and the

District of Columbia. It was founded in 1966 and its stated purpose is to "Take action through intersectional grassroots activism to promote feminist ideals, lead societal change, eliminate discrimination, and achieve and protect equal rights of all women and girls in all aspects of social, political and economic life." http://www.now.org/

New York Historical Society—For educators who cannot visit the New York Historical Society in New York, their site offers a wealth of information from their archive and an open course (fee based) in collaboration with Columbia University on women's history. https://www.nyhistory.org/womens-history

UN Women—A United Nations entity dedicated to gender equality and the empowerment of women. This organization was established to promote the progress of women's rights worldwide. They actively work with UN Member states to design laws, policies, programs, and services that will benefit women and girls worldwide. Their website has resources via their digital library that includes current data on the advancement of women and a list of publications. This is a useful site for those looking to take a deep dive into the issues affecting women across the globe. https://www.unwomen.org/en

She Should Run—This organization promotes leadership and encourages women from all walks of life to run for public office. Their goal is for 250,000 women to run for office by 2030. They believe that women with various political ideologies, ethnicities, and backgrounds should have the opportunity to lead in elected office so that democracies will benefit from different perspectives. They provide a toolkit, encouragement, and resources to help women begin their journey in running for political office. According to the organization, they have inspired over 21,000 women to run for office between 2016 and 2019. http://www.sheshouldrun.org/

National Women's History Alliance—This organization successfully lobbied Congress to designate March as National Women's History month. Leading the way, they establish a theme for women's history each year. They provide a wealth of research materials and resources for educational purposes and in celebration of women. Although starting with women's history month, this team now collaborates with other women's organizations to promote the study of women's history throughout the year. Their website is a valuable resource for teachers looking for background information and for students in their study of history and the role of women present in and omitted from standard textbooks. http://www.nationalwomenshistoryalliance.org/

Save the Children—This organization serves millions of children in the United States and around the world because children are not getting what they deserve. Save the Children reaches the most vulnerable children—those in need of food, an education, a home, or a safe place to live. This site can be used as a good resource for research statistics. For students working on fundraising opportunities, the organization accepts donations to send a child to school for a year. http://www.savethechildren.org/

See Jane—See Jane was founded in 2004 by actor Geena Davis. Their goal is to engage film industry professionals in a conversation about the creation of gender-balanced on-screen roles, reducing stereotypes, and raising awareness of the need for positive female roles for girls and women. This site has resources for educators developed with journalists, content creators, and teaching institutions to develop curriculum focused on gender equality. The statistics on gender and racial disparity of on-screen and behind-the-screen roles can provide opportunities to integrate gender and intersectionality discussion in upper elementary debate classes or as a means of podcast discussions or research projects. http://www.seejane.org/

The Representation Project—First came the film, *The Representation Project*; then, the organization by the same name was formed. This first film of three focused on the negative stereotyping of girls and women in society and shone a light on its impact. For educators looking for background information, personal stories, and educational data, this film provides all of that and inspiration to integrate this new understanding into current curriculum. The second film, *The Mask You Live In* focuses on the lives of boys as they navigate the narrow passage that is defined as manhood. Just like *The Representation Project*, *The Mask You Live In* has the power to not only educate educators but to also modify practices with this new understanding. The latest film, *The Great American Lie* tells the story of the ever-widening income gap through not only an economic lens, but through a gender one as well. http://www.therepresentationproject.org/

Lean In—Sheryl Sandburg gained a global reputation as a hard-pressing corporate executive and author of her book, *Lean In*. But her organization has a broader reach than just the corporate boardroom. Lean In leads women through education, activism, and pure inspiration. This site provides a wealth of resources that educators can pass along to their students. http://www.leanin.org/

Teach a Girl to Lead—This site from Rutgers University has curriculum developed through a gender lens. It includes inspirational stories, books, and videos about female leadership and activities and exercises. https://tag.rutgers.edu/

Teaching Tolerance—This site provides resources for educators, counselors, and parents of children from kindergarten through twelfth grade. Curriculum allows for the integration of social justice concepts, including the concept that children should be valued and respected without regard to their race, ethnicity, economic status, or gender. There is an emphasis on children as change agents. http://www.tolerance.org/

Chapter 10

FEMINISTS IN HISTORY

Bella Abzug, Betty Friedan, and Gloria Steinem are often credited with the twentieth-century feminist movement. Within the feminist movement, there are considered to be four movements. Abzug, Friedan, and Steinem belong to the second wave and most well-known today. The first wave, between 1848 and 1920, saw the passage of the Nineteenth Amendment through the work of abolitionists and feminists such as Sojourner Truth, Maria Stewart, and Frances E. W. Harper.

Bella Abzug—"At the age of 50, Abzug ran for congress in Manhattan and won on a strong feminist and peace platform. She quickly became a nationally known legislator, one of only 12 women in the House. Her record of accomplishments in Congress continually demonstrated her unshakable convictions as an anti-war activist and as a fighter for social and economic justice." https://jwa.org/womenofvalor/abzug

Betty Friedan—"Journalist, activist, and co-founder of the National Organization for Women, Betty Friedan was one of the early leaders of the women's rights movement of the 1960s and 1970s. Her 1963 best-selling book, The Feminine Mystique, gave voice to millions of American women's frustrations with their limited gender roles and helped spark widespread public activism for gender equality." https://www.womenshistory.org/education-resources/biographies/betty-friedan

Gloria Steinem—"Acclaimed journalist, trailblazing feminist, and one of the most visible, passionate leaders and spokeswomen of the women's rights movement in the late 20th and early 21st centuries." Steinem founded *Ms. Magazine*, a feminist monthly publication in 1971. https://www.womenshistory.org/education-resources/biographies/gloria-steinem

FOR GIRLS AND THE EDUCATORS WHO LEAD THEM

Ban Bossy—Sponsored by Lean In and Girl Scouts, this site encourages girls to ban the word *bossy* and to instead strengthen their leadership muscles. As girls grow into upper elementary and middle school years, many lose their confidence in being a leader. This site has tips for girls, parents, and teachers to help build confidence and skills to lead and to step outside of their comfort zone. http://www.banbossy.org/

Girl Rising—The Girl Rising team is committed to supporting the education of girls through the art of storytelling. They began with a film about nine girls, written by award-winning authors and voiced by Hollywood celebrities. Each segment is a moving tale of overcoming adversity and abuse and ultimately enduring and succeeding. The film has been translated into over thirty languages. Prescreening by educators is highly recommended before showing to upper elementary students. Some segments are more appropriate for this age group than others. In addition to the film, there is a *Girl Rising* film and curriculum that teachers can modify for time and age level. http://www.girlrising.org/

Girl Scouts of the USA—Whether students are interested in becoming a Girl Scout or just learning about the global impact girls can make, this site is a valuable resource. The Girl Scout organization has been around for over 100 years and in that time has committed to helping girls develop a strong sense of self, seek challenges, display values, nurture relationships, and solve community problems. On this site, girls can find positive role models and inspiration for their own missions in life. http://www.girlscouts.org/

Girl Up—This organization started as a campaign for American girls, but has transformed into one that supports girls across the globe. Their mission is to promote future girl leaders. For educators looking for ways to support leadership skills in upper elementary students, this organization provides the resources and inspiration. They have raised millions of dollars for United Nations programs that support the health and well-being of girls. http://www.girlup.org/

Girls Who Code—According to Girls Who Code, in 1995, 37 percent of computer scientists were women. By 2030, it is predicted that number will decrease to 22 percent. Girls Who Code Clubs are free after-school programs that include elementary girls in grades three to six. This is a sisterhood of role models and peers using computer science to advance girls and women in computer science and to change the world. Educators who are interested in forming a Girls Who Code club will find ample information on this site. http://www.girlswhocode.org/

FOR BOYS AND THE EDUCATORS WHO LEAD THEM

A Call to Men—This organization's goal is to train and educate men and boys to embrace and promote a healthy and respectful manhood. They describe their vision as creating a world where all men and boys are loving and respectful and all women and girls are valued and safe. The organization's leader, Ted Porter, also authored the book, *Breaking Out of the Man Box*, which describes the damaging effects of the socialization of men to be in control. For elementary educators, this site and book can deliver a perspective that has the power to influence classroom practices. http://www.acalltomen.org/

The Boy Crisis—The Boy Crisis site by author and psychologist Warren Farrell addresses the crisis of education, health, fathering, and purpose for boys. Many of the resources available are also in the book *The Boy Crisis*, by this author, who addresses a crisis in manhood that stems from the rearing of boy children. Boycrisis.org

The Boys Initiative—The goal of The Boys Initiative is to shed light on underachievement among boys and young men, to create dialogue and debate about it, and collaborate on solutions with those who are committed to the futures of our nation's youth. They seek to accomplish this mission building coalitions with groups that represent the interests of girls and women, boys and men, and parents and teachers and adolescent health care providers. This site's resources section contains the more useful information, with links to a variety of articles on boy's physical, emotional, and mental health. http://www.theboycrisis.org

Boys and Girls Club of America—The mission of the Boys and Girls Club is to enable all young people to reach their full potential and to become caring and productive citizens. Two programs that include elementary aged students are the Million Members, Million Hours of Service projects, and a leadership program called The Torch Club for children eleven to thirteen. The News and Stories section of this site contains a wealth of stories that not only serve as good information for educators but ones that can serve as inspiration to fuel service projects and social justice initiatives in classrooms and schools. https://www.bgca.org/

FOR GENDER-DIVERSE STUDENTS AND THE EDUCATORS WHO LEAD THEM

Gender Diversity—The mission of this organization is to increase awareness and understanding of the wide range of gender diversity in children through support, community building, and communication. There is information for educators about gender diversity in schools. http://www.genderdiversity.org

Gender Spectrum—Gender Spectrum provides community information and training on support for gender-variant children and their families. They also present the annual Gender Spectrum Family Conference for people raising gender-nonconforming, gender-variant, and transgender children and adolescents. http://www.genderspectrum.org/

Trans Youth Family Allies—TYFA's mission is to work toward creating a society free from violence and suicide and one in which all children are respected and celebrated. This site has educational information pertinent for elementary educators to support goals of eliminating harassment and oppression of transgender children. http://www.imatyfa.org/

Youth Report—The Youth Report is the Human Rights Campaign's report, Growing Up LGBT in America. This survey of more than 10,000 LGBT-identified children ages thirteen to seventeen provides a picture of the challenges and difficulties they face. For elementary educators, this report provides a window into the future of their own LGBT students and possible outcomes for them in middle and high school. https://www.hrc.org/youth-report

Trans Kid Purple Rainbow Foundation—TKPRF's mission is to support trans kids in their schools to ensure that they receive equal rights in a bully-free environment. Trans youth stories on this site provide a glimpse into the hearts and minds of trans kids as they face the challenges of leading a life that is so often poorly misunderstood. http://www.transkidspurplerainbow.org/

FOR STUDENTS FACING INTERSECTIONALITY AND THE EDUCATORS WHO LEAD THEM

Intersectionality Score Calculator—This site's calculator, while not completely inclusive of categories, provides a visual presentation on user's level of intersectionality. For educators, this can be a very effective way to determine the layers of implicit bias individual students in their schools are facing. https://intersectionalityscore.com/?from=g_keywords&keyword=intersectional&adposition=1o1&source=google&device=c&ad=2

"Kids Explaining Intersectionality"—This short YouTube video is a great introduction for elementary students to the term intersectionality. https://www.youtube.com/watch?v=WzbADY-CmTs

Intersectionality 101—This video is appropriate for a faculty meeting on implicit biases, a character education class, or as a social justice introduction for both adults and children. https://www.youtube.com/watch?v=w6dnj2IyYjE

Intersectionality Facts for Kids—This fact sheet is age appropriate for upper elementary. Adding a few comprehension questions at the end of this reading would enable educators to integrate an understanding of intersectionality into language arts lessons. https://kids.kiddle.co/Intersectionality

The Urgency of Intersectionality—In this powerful TED Talk video, Kimberlé Crenshaw explains in graphic detail the impact of intersectionality on black women. This video is a great primer for adults looking to learn more on the topic and to fully appreciate the impact of multiple biases for women. https://www.ted.com/talks/kimberle_crenshaw_the_urgency_of_intersectionality?language=en

FOR EDUCATORS TEACHING WOMEN'S HISTORY

National Women's History Museum—Their mission is to tell stories of women who transformed the U.S. educators would certainly benefit from a visit to the site of this museum in Arlington, Virginia, but the resources online are rich with information. They have a digital library with an easy search by topic and grade level. https://www.womenshistory.org

National Women's History Alliance—This organization's mission is to promote women's history and is committed to education, empowerment, equality, and inclusion. Of particular value for educators are articles on the centennial of the suffrage movement.

Women's History Month—This federal government site will excite educators who are looking to tap into the National Archives on women's history. It contains several complete lesson plans on key women in history such Rosa Parks and Eleanor Roosevelt as well as fascinating histories of artists including Mary Cassatt and Georgia O'Keefe. https://nationalwomenshistoryalliance.org/

EDUCATIONAL THEORISTS AND RESEARCHERS

When studying these theorists and researchers, educators may also integrate their new knowledge on the acquisition of gender biases or gender-healthy attitudes through their social, cultural, and community interactions. There are many other theorists' work to study. These four are included for theories that can support a gender-healthy environment.

Abraham Maslow—American psychologist whose theory of the hierarchy of needs describes individuals' growth toward fulfillment and self-actualization. As people progress in the hierarchy of needs (that others have placed in the well-known pyramid) they become more adept at feeling happiness through psychological health and creativity.

Lev Vygotsky—Soviet psychologist whose social development theory is widely studied in education. His theory stresses the fundamental role of social interaction in the development of cognition. He believed that children make meaning from what takes place in their community.

Benjamin Bloom—American psychologist who developed Bloom's Taxonomy. The framework developed by Bloom and his collaborators consisted of six major categories, one building upon the next. The original taxonomy has "knowledge" as the precondition for putting skills and abilities into practice. The revised taxonomy, produced by Lorin Anderson and other cognitive psychologists, has "remember" as the precondition for the subsequent skills and abilities. Note: Educators often use Bloom's pyramid in lesson development. Adding consideration of how gender factors into the analysis, evaluation, and creation processes can broaden opportunities created for students.

Maria Montessori—Italian physician and educator whose educational theory *The Absorbent Mind* describes methods for the way children learn naturally by absorbing all that is around them. There are thousands of Montessori schools worldwide. One of Montessori's central tenets is represented in this quote: "Joy, feeling one's own value, being appreciated and loved by others, feeling useful and capable of production are all factors of enormous value for the human soul."

OTHER PROFESSIONAL DEVELOPMENT RESOURCES

"Why Does Gender Matter? Counteracting Stereotypes With Young Children" by Olaiya E. Aina and Petronella A. Cameron. In this text, authors explore gender development theories and the influence of gender identity and stereotypes. https://pdfs.semanticscholar.org/ec27/5610d0ecbc1269a5f3a3ae8312b190a6977e.pdf

"The Insidiousness of Unconscious Bias in Schools" by Seth Gershenson and Thomas S. Dee. This article focuses on older children, but elementary teachers can easily place themselves and their students in corresponding roles and situations. https://www.brookings.edu/blog/brown-center-chalkboard/2017/03/20/the-insidiousness-of-unconscious-bias-in-schools/

"The Extraordinary Relevance of Girl's Schools" by Elizabeth F. Cleary—This article prompts educators to consider the qualities of single sex education and if they can be integrated into mixed gendered schools. https://www.womenshistory.org/articles/extraordinary-relevance-girls-schools

Creating Gender Inclusive Schools—This film depicts educational settings that welcome all young people regardless of how they identify on the gender identity spectrum. Free through library systems. See Kanopy link on site. https://www.newday.com/film/creating-gender-inclusive-schools

"Redraw the Balance"—This two-minute film has a powerful message about implicit bias in young children. Appropriate for adults and students. https://www.inspiringthefuture.org/redraw-the-balance/

The Danger of a Single Story—Chimamanda Ngosi Adichie tells the story of how she found her authentic cultural voice and warns that if we hear only a single story about another person or country, we risk missing critical pieces resulting in a different and inaccurate story. https://www.ted.com/talks/chimamanda_ngozi_adichie_the_danger_of_a_single_story

GENDERED-BRAIN RESEARCH VIDEOS

Gina Rippon—The Gendered Brain https://www.youtube.com/watch?v=wpPTpPvbcVo

Is Your Brain Male or Female https://www.youtube.com/watch?v=sSIEs1ngNiU

Sex Differences on Brain and Emotional Memory—Dr. Larry Cahill https://www.youtube.com/watch?v=IG5-yZdke48

GLOSSARY OF GENDER AND RELATED TERMS

Ally—A person who is not LGBTQ but shows support for LGBTQ people and promotes equality.

Androgynous—Identifying and/or presenting as neither masculine nor feminine.

Asexual—A lack of a sexual desire for other people of any gender.

Biphobia prejudice—A fear or hatred of bisexual people.

Bisexual—A person attracted to more than one sex, gender, or gender identity.

Cisgender—A person whose gender identity corresponds with the sex assigned to them at birth.

Closeted—An LGBTQ person who has not disclosed their sexual orientation or gender identity.

Coming out—The process in which a people first shares with others their sexual orientation or gender identity.

Gay—A person who is emotionally, romantically, or sexually attracted to members of the same gender.

Gender dysphoria—Clinically significant distress caused when a person's assigned birth gender is not the same as the one with which they identify.

Gender equity—When people of any gender or gender identification enjoy the same rights, resources, opportunities, and protections.

Gender expansive—A wider range of gender identity and/or expression than usually associated with the binary gender system.

Gender expression—External appearance of one's gender identity, usually expressed through behavior and outward appearance.

Gender fluid—A person who does not identify with having a fixed gender identification.

Gender identity—One's innermost concept of self as male or female, blend of both or neither—how individuals perceive themselves.

Gender nonconforming—People who do not behave in a way that conforms to the traditional expectations of their gender.

Gender transition—The process by which some people change so that they feel more closely aligned with their internal understanding of gender with their outward appearance. This can be done through the changing of names, dress, or use of pronouns or by undergoing physical transitions to modify their bodies.

Gender—The social construct of roles, behaviors, and attributes of individuals and groups. Gender interacts with, but is different from, binary categories of biological sex.

Genderqueer—Genderqueer people typically reject typical categories of gender and embrace a fluidity of gender identity and often, though not always, sexual orientation.

Homophobia—Discomfort, fear, or hatred of people who are attracted to members of the same sex.

Intersex—A broad range of natural variations of the body. In some cases, these traits are visible at birth and, in other cases, not until puberty. Some variations never become visible.

Lesbian—A woman who is emotionally, romantically, or sexually attracted to other women.

LGBTQ—An acronym for lesbian, gay, bisexual, transgender, and queer.

Nonbinary—A person who does not identify exclusively as a man or a woman.

Outing—Exposing someone's lesbian, gay, bisexual, or transgender identity to others without their permission.

Pansexual—Someone who may have emotional, romantic, or sexual attraction to people of any gender.

Queer—A term people often use to describe fluid identities and orientations.

Questioning—People who are in the process of exploring their sexual orientation or gender identity.

Same-gender loving—A term some prefer to use instead of lesbian, gay, or bisexual to express love and attraction to persons of the same gender.

Self-concepts—An individual's perceptions of own behavior, abilities, and characteristics.

Self-efficacy—An individual's belief in own ability to succeed in specific situations. A person's sense of self-efficacy can play a major role in how a person approaches goals and challenges.

Self-esteem—An individual's overall feeling of value or worth.

Sex assigned at birth—The sex given to a child at birth, most often based on the child's external anatomy.

Sexual orientation—An inherent and consistent emotional, romantic, or sexual attraction to other people.

Stereotype threat—The psychological threat that arises when a person is in a situation for which a negative stereotype about one's group applies.

Transgender—People whose gender identity or expression is different from cultural expectations based on the sex they were assigned at birth. Transgender people may also identify as straight, gay, lesbian, or bisexual.

Transphobia—Discomfort, fear, or hatred of transgender people.

Index

A Call to Men, 65, 116, 125
absorbent mind, 3, 8
Abzug, Bella, 124
action plans, 5, 36, 46–50, 61–62
Adichie, Chimamanda Ngozi, 129
advertising: biased messaging, 13, 99; non-biased messaging, 65, 73, 86
Aina, Olaiya E., 57, 129
Arnett, Jeffrey J., 67
Aronson, Joshua, 108
art teachers, as members of gender study teams, 34
assessments/surveys: character education, through, 28–30; differentiating, 26; independent evaluations, 37–39; authorizing environment, 62, 63; L&L Classroom Layout & Design, 18–19; L&L Curriculum/Literature Survey, 19–21; L&L Educator Self-Reflection Survey, 24–26; L&L Instructional Language/Behaviors Survey, 21–24

behavior: bias and, 11–12, 57; controlling boys, 18, 24; frameworks for, 2, 3; gender differences and, 5–6, 67; gender expression and, 4; gender expectations and, 5; intersectionality, impact of, 58, 111; nutrition, influences, 108, 118; survey and assessments of, 21, 38; teachers and community, 37, 43–45, 50, 60, 61

Bian, Lin, 14
bias: children's beliefs, 14, 15, 39, 57; confirmation bias, 7, 24; educators' beliefs, 15, 18, 24, 39, 40, 57, 109, 111, 115; families, 63, 64; freedom from, 15, 17, 24; language, and, 101, 103; layers of (intersectionality), 14, 58, 68, 101, 106–108; school system, and, 14, 40, 57, 60, 61; student performance, result of, 85, 110
Black Girls Matter: Pushed Out, Overpoliced and Underprotected, 106
Bloom, Benjamin, 5, 109
The Boy Crisis, 65, 116, 125
Boys and Girls Club of America, 106
The Boys Initiative, 126
brain: genetically based differences, 5–8; learning theories, and, 55; lessons for students, 82–83, 98–99, 115; processing information, 114–115
Brookings Institute, study on gender bias, 12

Cahill, Larry, 5, 121
California framework on sex education, 104
Cameron, Petronella A., 129
character education, 28–32, 69, 127
Classroom Layout and Design Survey, 18–19
Cleary, Elizabeth F., 58

cognitive development: abilities, 5, 6; learning, and, 45, 110; biopsychosocial perspective, 6–7
collaborative intention, 3, 115
community participation,: participation, 63, 64–66, 105, 106; stakeholders, 61, 62
Creating Gender Inclusive Schools, 4, 56, 129
Crenshaw, Kimberle Williams, 14, 106, 107, 127
Curriculum/Literature Survey, 19–21

The Danger of a Single Story, 57, 129
Daniels, Gilbert S., 9
Dee, Thomas S., 57

Educator Self-Reflection Survey, 24–26
Educators Code of Ethics, 43–45
ergodic theory, 10
The Extraordinary Relevance of Girl's Schools, 58

faculty and team meetings, facilitating, 55, 60
Farrell, Dr. Warren, 12, 65, 116
Friedan, Betty, 124
Film, *Creating Gender Inclusive Schools*, 4, 56, 129
Film, *Girl Rising*, 46, 59, 65, 87, 124
Film, *Inspire the Future - Redraw the Balance*, 49, 57, 65, 129
Film, *The Danger of a Single Story*, 57, 129
For Families: 5 Tips for Preventing and Reducing Gender Bias, 64

Gardner, Howard, 8–9
Gender Equity Champions, 46
gender expression, 4, 130
gender fluidity, 14, 116–105
gender identity, 1, 5, 14, 54, 104, 105, 111
gender health, 3, 15, 18, 26, 39, 40, 41, 42, 43, 51, 59, 115, 118
gender identity and language, 21, 24, 25, 50, 101–103
gender messages, 4, 17
gender pay gap, 97, 114
gender-based brain differences, 5–8

Gender Diversity Organization, 126
Gender Spectrum Organization, 126
Gershenson, Seth, 57, 129
giftedness, 5–6
Girl Rising, 46–50, 59, 65, 69, 90, 124
Girl Scouts of the USA, 125
Girl Up, 46–48, 69
Girls Who Code, 125

Halpern, Diane F., 6, 121
Hierarchy of Needs: Maslow, 29, 117, 128; freedom from gender limitations, 29–30, 31, 128; Traditional Male Hero's Values, 116–117
Hoff Sommers, Christina, 58
Human Rights Campaign Youth Report, 126

Implicit Bias Test/Project Implicit, 57
Individuals with Disabilities Act, 109
The Insidiousness of Unconscious Bias in Schools, 57
Inspire the Future - Redraw the Balance, 49, 57, 65, 129
Instructional Language/Behaviors Survey, 21–24, 25
International Day of the Girl, 19
International Rescue Fund, 49
International Space Station, 9
International Olympiad Math Challenge, 6
intersectionality: definition and impact, 14, 50, 58, 68, 103, 110–111; gender fluidity, 104–105; girls with disabilities, 2, 109; girls and racism, 106–107; racism, 108; score calculator, 127; socioeconomic status, 108

language and behavior survey, 21–24, 25
language, gender vocabulary, 103–104
Lean In, 123
lessons, students: activity preferences, 74–76; bias, 76–78, 80–82, 85–87; brain science, 82–83, 98–99; careers, 91–92; feminist movement/history, 92–98; gender characteristics, 78–79; personal choices, 71–73, 79–78; social/emotional understanding, 73, 87–91
librarians, library media specialists, 40
listening and looking tours, 33–34, 53

literature review, 41

The Mask You Live In, 123
Maslow, Abraham, 2–4, 29, 59, 117, 128
mathematics and gender, 6, 7, 9, 12, 38–39, 44, 49, 83
Montessori, Maria, 3, 8, 128
Moore, Mark, 61
multiple intelligences, theory of, 8
music teachers, as members of gender study teams, 98
Myth of Average, 9–10, 110–111

NASA, 9–10
National Center for Transgender Equality, 103
National Education Association (NEA), framework of ethical understandings, 43
National Women's History Alliance, 128
National Women's History Museum, 127
National Organization for Women, 121
Nature vs. Nurture, 5
neuroplasticity, 6–7
neuroscience, 5, 6–7, 8–9, 10–11
New York City "Guidelines for Supporting Transgender and Gender Expansive Students," 105
New York Historical Society, women's history, 6–7
Newman, Tim, 122
nonbinary: identification, 4; vocabulary, 103–105

parents: gender equity partners, 41–42, 53, 61–62, 65; gender stereotyping, 63; greater community, part of, 63–64, 118; rights and responsibilities, 30, 68, 104–105; social decision making, 4, 30, 44, 51
patriarchy, 15
physical education teachers, as members of gender study teams, 40, 98
Porter, Tony, 65
poverty, 3, 46, 87, 101–106, 108–110, 115
problem solving and negotiating, 61
professional development, 17–24, 39, 51, 55, 66, 67

race-based disparities and stressors, 108
Radical Collaboration, 60–61
Real Boys, 116
Real, Terence, 7
Representation Project, The, 123
Rose, Todd, 9

Save the Children, survey, 14
School Reform Initiative, 56
self-actualization, 4, 30, 116–118, 128
self-awareness, 19
self-concepts, 8, 13, 17, 28, 32, 45, 108, 131
self-efficacy, 1, 2, 8, 10–11, 30, 111
self-esteem, 2, 4, 17, 18, 45–46
seventh generation principle, 13
Sex and Gender: What's the Difference?, 56
sex education, framework and guidelines, 104
social-emotional health: families, 30, 41–42; socialization, and, 8, 30, 67–68, 68–69, 125
social media, 13, 42, 65
socioeconomic status, 14, 101, 108
society and culture, 10, 14, 15, 19, 61, 62, 67, 121, 123
special education, bias in referral, 109, 110
Steele, Claude, 108
Steinem, Gloria, 124
STEM, 30, 32–33
stereotypes, 21, 33–34, 50, 57–58, 64, 65, 111
stereotype threat, 2, 108, 113, 116
strategic action plan, 62, 63
strategic triangle, 61, 63
student motivation, 108
students: as change agents, 48–50; as role models, 42; mixed-age and mixed-gender opportunities, 42–43
students, lessons: activity preferences, 74–76; bias, 76–78, 80–82, 85–87; brain science, 82–83, 98–99; careers, 91–92; feminist movement/history, 92–93, 93–98; gender characteristics, 78–79; personal choices, 71–73, 79–78; social/emotional understanding, 73, 87–91
suicide rates, 11, 116

Teaching Tolerance, 123
team charter, 53
teams: assessments/evaluations, 17, 26, 32, 37; leading, 55, 63
Title IX law, 105
Trans Kid Purple Rainbow Foundation, 127
Trans Youth Family Allies, 126

UN Women, 122
The Urgency of Intersectionality, 58
U.S. Census, 114

U.S. Dept. of Education Office of Civil Rights, 106–107

Vgotsky, Lev, 3, 59, 128
visual culture, 34, 35, 59

wage gap, 114, 123
Why Does Gender Matter? Counteracting Stereotypes with Young Children, 57
Women's History Month, 19, 94, 122, 128
World Health Organization, 56

About the Author

Dorothy Chiffriller Venditto has served as an elementary teacher across all grade levels. Ms. Venditto is the recipient of the Empire State Teacher of Excellence Award and the Certificate in Advanced Educational Leadership from Harvard. She has published articles on academic success, school-wide enrichment, and gender equity in the classroom. Ms. Venditto has created workshops and classes on gender equity for both educators and students. Her certifications include elementary, middle school social studies, and national board certification for middle childhood. She recently founded a professional development company, Enlightened Schools, to provide educational opportunities that support the creation of gender-healthy school environments.

www.ingramcontent.com/pod-product-compliance
Lightning Source LLC
Chambersburg PA
CBHW030141240426
43672CB00005B/220